THE ENEMY IS
NEVER WRONG

THE ENEMY IS
NEVER WRONG

*Martial Art, Activism, and the
Fight for a Functional Future*

FRANK FORENCICH

ISBN (paperback) 978-0-9851263-7-7

ISBN (e-book) 978-0-9851263-8-4

Published by Exuberant Animal, Bend, Oregon

EXUBERANTANIMAL.COM

Resistance is not only about battling the forces of darkness. It is about becoming a whole and complete human being. It is about overcoming estrangement. It is about the capacity to love. It is about honoring the sacred. It is about dignity. It is about sacrifice. It is about courage. It is about being free. Resistance is the pinnacle of human existence.

Chris Hedges

It's 3:23 in the morning and I'm awake
because my great great grandchildren won't let me sleep
my great great grandchildren ask me in dreams
what did you do while the planet was plundered?
what did you do when the earth was unraveling?

surely you did something

when the seasons started failing?

as the mammals, reptiles, birds were all dying?

did you fill the streets with protest

when democracy was stolen?

What did you do once you knew?

    Drew Dellinger

CONTENTS

FOREWORD

The environmentalist and feminist writer Lierre Keith has written, "If there's anyone left alive 100 years from now, they are going to ask what was wrong with us, that we didn't fight like hell when the world was going down."

There can be no more important topics than how, when, where, why, and in what forms we resist. And Frank Forencich has written an important book about these topics. And even more importantly, he has written a clear and concise book about how we can *start* this resistance, moving from bemoaning the state of the world to actually doing something about it.

One of the smartest decisions of my life came because I wasn't paying enough for gas. I was in my mid-twenties, and I knew this culture was killing the planet. I knew the problems we face are overwhelming and immense. And I had absolutely no idea what to do about any of it.

So I decided that for every dollar I spent on gas I would give a dollar to a local environmental organization. But since I didn't have any money, I could instead pay myself $5/hour to do activism. So if I spent ten bucks on gas, I'd do two hours of activism.

I've always loved Florence Nightingale's famous line, "I attribute my success to this—I never gave or took any excuse." I started with letters to the editor. I was too scared to put my name into the public, but I wasn't going to let that excuse stop me. Then I started doing some anti-circus demonstrations. I knew circuses are horrible, but I didn't know details. So I'd show up at the demonstration, someone would hand me a sign, and if one of the circus-goers asked what's wrong with circuses, I'd shrug, point to the guy next to me, and say, "Ask him."

I did demonstrations against nuclear weapons, and against wearing fur. I recognized that these demonstrations didn't really accomplish much, but I didn't let myself use that as an excuse. Then I started doing timber sale appeals: trying to stop the Forest Service from deforesting public lands. Week in and week out, month in and month out, however much gas I used, that was how much activism I did. No excuses given or taken.

Another of the most important decisions came because a friend chewed me out. He told me that a gift from the universe comes with a responsibility and said that if you've been given a gift and you don't use that gift in the service of your community, then, to use his phrase, "you aren't worth shit." He was right. That was the night I dedicated my life to writing.

The third of these most important decisions came out of fear. Because even after all this, I still wasn't writing. I'd make all sorts of excuses—repeatedly disappointing the ghost of Florence Nightingale. There were plenty of reasons for the fear, all of them boiling down to one: I was abused as a child.

Here's what I mean. My writing has always been more personal, more emotional. I identified with a quote I read when I was young, about how easy writing is: all you do is tap a vein and write using your own blood.

But I couldn't do that. I would sit, pen in hand, frozen, feeling a hollowness inside where feelings should be. Then I realized I was feeling much the same dread I'd felt as a child, sitting on the couch, trying not to be noticed by my abusive father. After that, I realized I had a choice: I could go the rest of my life with the best excuse in the world for not following my dream or I could do whatever it took to live the life I was supposed to be living.

And finally, the best piece of advice I ever received concerning writing (or life, or social change) came before I was born. My mother had a close and moving relationship with her grandmother. She used to visit her almost every day, even at four and five years old, walking across the pastures from her parents' home to her grandparents'. Something her grandmother used to say to her often, and my mother then said to me, is, "Inch by inch, life's a cinch. Yard by yard, life is hard."

I know it's a cliché, but it's true. Writing a book is intimidating. If I think about it, I'll sit here and do nothing. But I can write a page. And then another page. And then another. And before you know it, I have a book.

Likewise, the problems we face in this world feel overwhelming and insoluble. This culture is waging war against the planet, against women, against children. And the momentum of these wars is far too fierce to stop. We have no chance. And if there's no chance, we may as well just party like there's no tomorrow. Or maybe we just enjoy what we can. Or maybe we just grieve the loss of the world we are doing nothing to save.

But we don't, to switch metaphors, swallow the monster all in one bite. We can't. We're not superheroes whose superpower is ever-expanding gullets. We're just human beings with gifts, gifts we need to use in the service of our communities.

The big distinction, it seems to me, is not between those who believe we need to tear down the entire system and those who believe we can reform it. The big distinction is between those who do something and those who don't.

When the United States invaded Iraq in 2003, writer Dahr Jamail was living and working in Alaska. He didn't like how the corporate media was covering the invasion, but instead of just complaining about this coverage, he decided to do a better job. He went to Iraq and started writing better and more honest stories.

Sherrie Tippie cuts hair for a living. And she really likes beavers. Beavers are extraordinarily important to streams and rivers in almost every way imaginable: ponds behind beaver dams are some of the most biodiverse habitat in the world. She got tired of hearing about Colorado state wildlife officials killing beavers in places where people didn't want them. Instead of just complaining about the killings of these beavers and the destruction of these streams, she did something about it. For the last twenty years she has been live-trapping unwanted beavers in the greater Denver area and relocating them to streams in need of beavers. By now she's nationally recognized for her expertise in trapping and re-locating beaver.

Maria Diekmann was born in the United States but has spent more than half her life in Namibia. She loves the wildlife there, especially lesser known creatures like pangolins. Pangolins are small armored mammals who primarily eat ants and termites. They're delightful creatures. They're the most trafficked nonhuman animal in the world, primarily killed because some people believe that eating their shells improves a man's ability to maintain an erection. The shells are simply keratin, so the men would do just as well to chew their own fingernails.

Diekmann works with anti-poaching organizations and the police in several nations to protect pangolins. She's also one of the few pangolin rehabilitators in the world, nursing pangolins back to health who have been rescued from poachers, then releasing them into the wild.

A few days ago I received an email from a woman who told me that developers wanted to cut down an ancient maple tree because it "intruded" on their parking lot. "I told them the tree had landmark status and it was illegal to harm it" she wrote. "They asked if I had documentation and I said, 'Of course. See you in court, and you're going to look horrible when I tell the judge you're harassing a senior citizen over a tree protected as a landmark.' We had a few screaming battles and my neighbors joined the fight. The developers backed down and the beautiful tree still stands. After it was all over, one of my neighbors stopped by and said 'That whole story was bullshit wasn't it?' And I said of course you can't landmark a tree." I have a new hero.

And I have a new favorite book, which happens to be the one you're holding in your hands.

Derrick Jensen is a co-author of *Bright Green Lies* and the author of *The Myth of Human Supremacy, Endgame, The Culture of Make Believe*, and *A Language Older than Words*. Democracy Now! has called him "the poet-philosopher of the ecology movement."

WELCOME TO THE FIGHT

How are you feeling right now? How's your mind-body-spirit coping with the demands of the modern world? Are you coming to grips with the challenges of our time, or are you struggling to find your way?

If you're like most people, you're probably feeling pretty uneasy if not downright anxious. In fact, there's a good chance that you're feeling stressed, maybe depressed, even terrified. Stress and wicked problems are everywhere now: international conflicts, rampaging viruses, economic injustice, systemic racism, battles over women's reproductive rights, school shootings, misinformation, and threats to democracy itself. Every day we hear about declining levels of social trust, polarization, gridlock, and bad behavior at the highest levels of government. And looming above it all, a sense of imminent ecological collapse, the most serious crisis that humanity has ever faced.

You try to carry on with your so-called normal life, but the effort feels increasingly onerous and maybe even absurd. You feel cornered by chaos, confusion, and stress—and behind it all, the sneaking suspicion that something is fundamentally wrong with people, society, or modern culture. You want your life to matter, and you'd like to be relevant, but there's so much to do, and you don't know where or how to begin. Your mind is racing trying to make sense of it all, and sometimes it feels like you're drowning in complexity. *What can one person possibly do to move the needle on the state of the world?*

LIFE UNDER SIEGE

It all feels so intimidating now, so bleak and menacing. Every time we turn around, we hear yet another story about a failing biosphere and dysfunctional human systems. The headlines overwhelm us: "We're in the sixth mass extinction," "Chemical pollution has passed safe limit for humanity," "Greenland ice cap loses enough water in 20 years to cover US," "Fossil fuel companies have humanity by the throat," "New report suggests 'High Likelihood of Human Civilization Coming to an End' starting in 2050." It's no wonder that some people now refer to young people as "Generation Dread."

Even the uninformed can feel the ecological noose tightening. Every day we hear phrases like "ecological overshoot," "hothouse Earth," "planetary toxification," "carbon bombs," "ecocide," and "biospheric tipping points" that will soon be crossed or may have already been crossed. A series of highly credible scientific reports describe an imminent, existential threat to civilization. Books such as *The Uninhabitable Earth* by David Wallace-Wells predict a harsh future and tell us, "No matter how well-informed you are, you are surely not alarmed enough."

The stakes couldn't possibly be higher. Sober climate scientists tell us that early projections were too conservative and that the planetary emergency we're seeing today is considerably worse than predicted. They warn of a "flammable future" that is "fundamentally incompatible with agriculture." Updated projections are simply dire. As one eminent climate scientist put it, "We're putting our kids onto a global school bus that will with 98% probability end in a deadly crash." We try to press on and deny the reality, but our defenses are wearing thin.

In conventional settings, we're encouraged to keep our heads down, work hard, and keep a positive attitude, but it all sounds increasingly hollow, even nonsensical. If you're a young person, or even an adult in mid-career, you're confronted by a monstrous paradox: even if you do manage to jump through all the hoops of achievement and become a conventional "success," you're still going to be living in a world on the brink of planetary-scale catastrophe. In a few short years, entire regions of our planet may become uninhabitable or highly degraded. And what good is it to succeed in wealth and prestige when your world is poisoned beyond recognition?

To make matters worse, we're beginning to lose confidence in the prevailing cultural narratives that formerly gave us a sense of meaning, purpose, and direction. To put it bluntly, *our stories no longer work*. Familiar narratives of capitalism, individualism, "man over nature," and progress sound increasingly hollow. We look elsewhere for useful stories, but in the meantime, we're left with a vague sense of floating in space; the narrative ground beneath our feet no longer supports us.

If you're a young person, you're probably furious to learn that your elders are leaving you a toxic mess of wicked problems that you're expected to clean up and put in order. But no matter your age, the future looms large, posing a thousand urgent questions about who we are, how to behave, and what we might become. We try to ignore our predicament, and sometimes we succeed for a day or two, but it always seems to come roaring back, bigger and more threatening than ever.

The numbers tell a disturbing story. In 2021, the American Academy of Pediatrics issued a "Declaration of a National Emergency in Child and Adolescent Mental Health." A 2022 report by the medical journal *Lancet Planetary Health* found that "75% of respondents said that they think the future is frightening." Also in 2022, the *Healthy Minds Study* at UCLA reported that "depression, anxiety, and suicidal thoughts have doubled in the last decade." Clearly something is very wrong with our planet, our minds, and our spirits—a condition that reverberates in the state of our bodies. As the ecopsychologist Theodore Roszak famously put it, "The earth hurts and we hurt with it."

In our pain and frustration, we turn to counselors and ecotherapists who specialize in human relationships with nature, but relief is fleeting and difficult to grasp. We're advised to "turn outrage into action," but what action is that? Protest on the street? Write letters? Become militant? Start a nonprofit organization? What actually moves the world? Greta Thunberg tells us to act "as if your house is on fire," but most of us don't even know where to begin.

MAGICAL THINKING

You might suppose that, given the fact that decisive action is essential to our survival, modern society would be eager to embrace an educational curriculum that offers the skills, knowledge, and perspectives that would help us find our way to a functional and sustainable future. But sadly, we have almost nothing to show in this respect. Most of us receive little or no training in activism or conflict. We don't know how to fight, when to fight, what to fight, or even why to fight. Likewise, few of us receive any education on the fundamentals of danger and risk. To put it another way, most of us have no idea how to be effective agents for change.

You probably remember how it went when you were a kid. If your family was typical, your mother said, "Don't fight," but your father said, "Don't lose." And when it came to making a difference in the world, the only advice your teachers could offer was, "Be sure to vote." And that was the end of it.

But with all due respect to Mom, Dad, and the other adults in our lives, this simplistic advice is little help in a hypercomplex world that's teetering on the edge of social and ecological collapse. Conflict is everywhere, but rarely do we teach it in any intentional or systematic way. We avoid the issue, deny the reality, and hope for the best. Quite obviously, this is not a formula for success.

In essence, we're in denial about the reality of conflict and the state of the world. You might even say that our culture is in the grip of magical thinking—we seem to believe that untrained young people will somehow grow up and instinctively do the right thing in the face of hyper-complex challenges, adversity, and conflict. But this expectation is preposterous. If someone suggested that we drop untrained young people into any other high-demand environment—professional sports, medicine, law, first responder work, aviation—we would rightly call them out for being delusional.

In fact, there's a yawning gap in our culture, an educational blind spot. We don't like conflict, and we're inclined to view fighting as an aberration, an occasional incident, and a failure of normal social living. It's a glitch in human affairs, a bug in the system. So we wring our hands and look the other way, hoping things will work themselves out. But the absence of a conflict curriculum is far more than a simple oversight; it's a tragic, life-threatening omission and a form of educational malpractice.

Perhaps it's no wonder. After all, our culture has wildly divergent, contradictory attitudes about conflict and engagement. On the one hand, fighting is often dismissed as uncivilized, barbaric, uncouth, and unacceptable. Fighting is for people who lack emotional control and, in this sense, it's often viewed as a personal failure. On the other hand, our heroes are often presented as one-dimensional warriors. Action-adventure movies feature invulnerable protagonists whose primary skill is the ability to deliver punches and dominate opponents. And they always win in the end.

Caught between these absurdities, it's no wonder we flounder. We feel conflicted about fighting, so we lurch clumsily from one encounter to the next, struggling to find our footing. And when things go wrong, we're quick to blame ourselves for our awkwardness and incompetence. *I feel confused, defeated, and ineffective...there must be something wrong with me.* But, more likely, there's nothing wrong with you at all; what you really need is training, practice, and perspective.

EIGHT BILLION WHITE BELTS

Our failure to educate ourselves about action and engagement has serious consequences that ripple through every human system. Untrained fighters swing wildly from one pole to the other. Some become passive victims while others overreact and leave a trail of ugliness in their wakes. Many waste valuable time fighting the wrong battles against the wrong opponents. These fighters are not only ineffective in their activism, they also gum up the works and make everyone else miserable.

This failure leads to bad behavior in a thousand forms. Some of us become bullies and attack people or countries without provocation. We stockpile arms and build walls of all kinds: physical, legal, and psychological. We fight whatever's handy, and if nothing's handy, we invent adversaries out of thin air. We imagine ourselves as powerless victims and blame imaginary perpetrators for our troubles. We go in search of rescue by people, substances, organizations, or ideologies. And, not surprisingly, all this behavior is highly contagious and wickedly counterproductive.

Given our lack of education, it's not surprising that most of us don't know the fundamentals of activism—the who, what, where, when, and how of making a difference. You've probably wondered: Should I go on a school strike? Go to law school and run for office? Work inside the system or outside it? Should I vandalize construction equipment like George Hayduke in Edward Abbey's *The Monkey Wrench Gang*? Become an eco-pirate like Paul Watson of the Sea Shepherd Conservation Society? Should I practice civil disobedience, or should I meditate, adjust, and adapt? And, most of all, what kind of relationship should I hold with the world around me?

All of which adds up to a disturbing and immensely challenging big-picture perspective. That is, the planet is now home to nearly eight billion humans, most of whom are living in a state of chronic stress, ambiguity, or outright fear.

And yet, we have essentially no education or training in activism, strategy, or martial philosophy. In fact, we might well say that our planet is now inhabited by eight billion white belts—inept, untrained primates trying desperately to create some kind of habitable world. This is not a recipe for success.

THE CASE FOR MARTIAL ARTISTRY

As a people, we're confused about fighting, engagement, and action. We see conflict as an aberration and a failure of normal social functioning. If only people would stop fighting, we could get back to our regular lives and all would be well. But what if fighting, far from being an occasional inconvenience, is intrinsic to the human condition? What if activism is fundamental to the objective of being a good social animal? And what if skillful fighting is actually essential to our sense of meaning, health, and social progress?

Like it or not, fighting is inevitable. No matter your personal ideology or belief system, any effort towards meaningful change is going to bring you up against entrenched interests and the inertia of the status quo. This is precisely the challenge we face on the level of planetary health, climate change, biodiversity, and survival. In popular conversations about our predicament, common recommendations typically go towards policy, law, and culture. We say that we need to nationalize fossil fuel companies or stop new fossil fuel projects. We need to protect vast areas of habitat and transform industrial agriculture. We need to tax the rich, establish universal health care, and cancel student loans. We need to enact programs that promote social justice and equality.

These proposals have merit, but all of them go against the grain of society-as-usual, which is to say, they all involve conflict. If we're going to create a new, viable future, we're going to have to change established organizations, institutions, and ways of living and working. And we're going to have to challenge the people and organizations who're profiting off of conventional practices.

WHY MARTIAL ART?

To have a shot at a functional future, we're going to need better fighters, people who understand the nature of conflict and are willing to engage. We need smart, sensitive, courageous people who can remain calm, effective, creative, and adaptable in the face of adversity. In other words, we're going to need martial artists.

All of which may well sound surprising. On the face of it, things like climate change, habitat destruction, and social injustice seem to have little or nothing to do with the challenges of hand-to-hand combat or battlefield strategy. But the time has come to expand our thinking to include a broader practice of acting, being, and relating to the world.

Just to be clear, this call for martial artistry is not about becoming an invulnerable warrior or an alpha primate. It's about understanding the world, being effective, and creating a healthy relationship with reality. It's about participation, engagement, and right action. It's about focus. It's about fighting with greater foresight and sensitivity to context. It's about how we stand and how we touch the world. It's about being relevant.

To be sure, martial artistry is about fighting, but since conflict is woven into the fabric of human experience, it's also about the art of living. In fact, martial artistry can and should be an essential part of a whole human curriculum, just as valid as any other academic subject, perhaps even more so. After all, what good is it to know a mountain of facts if you don't know how to deploy that knowledge in service of some larger objective?

BENEFITS OF A MARTIAL EDUCATION

Superficially, it might seem that martial art skills would only be valuable in exceptional circumstances, when the world closes in and threatens our bodies, our lives, or those of the people around us. But in fact, the benefits of a martial education extend to the deepest reaches of our experience. With training and reflection, we begin to think more clearly about our encounters, our relationships, our purposes, objectives, and strategies. Once you start asking the right questions about your struggles, you'll find yourself wasting less time on trivial annoyances, distractions, and petty battles. You'll focus more intently on what really matters.

In fact, martial artistry is about more than protecting ourselves and others. It's about more than winning battles or achieving victory. That's because, at its root, fighting is— or can be—an intensely educational process. No matter the outcome of our engagement, we learn. Every encounter teaches us—or should teach us—something important about the world and ourselves. We learn about power, the nature of people and organizations, our capabilities and our weaknesses. We learn about the content of our character.

Even better, engagement is good for our health. In conventional conversations, most of us are inclined to think of fighting as something stressful and even dangerous. But when our action is linked to a sense of meaning and purpose, we enter into a virtuous circle in which engagement becomes a vital element of healthy and successful living. We might even think of activism as a form of medicine in its own right. In recent years, a robust body of scientific research has shown that a sense of meaning and purpose has a powerful, salutary effect on the body and the mind. And when we reinforce that sense of meaning and purpose with action, we promote integration and, in turn, our health.

OUR UNCONVENTIONAL BATTLE

A martial education is valuable for anyone in any walk of life, and we can all benefit from traditional teachings. But it's all the more vital today because of our situation is so unique. With the fate of the biosphere hanging in the balance, we're now engaged in a highly unconventional, unprecedented, and unfamiliar battle for survival.

In a conventional fight, we're usually up against a well-defined adversary, an easily identified individual or group that we can focus on: The tribe on the other side of the river has attacked us, and we need to rally our forces and fight back. In this sense at least, conventional fighting is easy; your adversary might well be powerful, dangerous, and devious, but at least you we know who he is.

But today's fight for planetary survival is an unconventional, historically unprecedented kind of battle. Our adversaries are sometimes difficult to identify and grasp. They're often amorphous, diffuse, and widely distributed across humanity, organizations, policies, and culture. Battle lines are blurry and indistinct; we're often confused about where or what to fight, and we're not even sure what victory would look like. How do we fight back against massively embedded forces like growthism, vulture capitalism, runaway technology, or cultural imperialism? None of this is obvious.

To be sure, we do face some genuinely toxic adversaries and planet-hostile actors that must be opposed with legal and cultural force. But it's also true that our troubles are embedded in human nervous systems, habit, culture, and history. In a sense, we are all perpetrators in the destruction of the planet. Unless you're living an authentic hunting and gathering life in the outback, you've got a hand in the degradation of the biosphere. In other words, there's more to this predicament than a few bad actors—this is a systemic crisis that's distributed across the planet. And when "the enemy is us," as is so often said, we're called to a higher and more sophisticated kind of action. It's no longer enough to simply focus our opposition on some notorious "other"; we need to be skillful, sophisticated, and introspective as well.

THE JOURNEY TO FOCUS

With each passing year, more and more people are coming to grips with our ecosocial crisis and looking for a path forward. Everyone responds differently, but in general, the journey to activism comes in three stages, each one defined by how we react to the great encounter of our era and the dawning realization that we are in serious, epic, and catastrophic trouble. How will we respond once we're exposed to "the knowledge"? How will we behave when we come to realize the depth, magnitude, and urgency of our predicament?

STAGE 1: OUR SO-CALLED "NORMAL" LIFE

The first stage of our journey is marked by various levels of ignorance, denial, and passivity. In this phase, we're content with the status quo and satisfied with culture-as-usual. We're dimly aware of problems at the perimeter of our lives, but it's pretty easy to brush them aside and carry on with our familiar routines. When we're confronted by issues like climate change, social injustice, and the destruction of the biosphere, we're quick to fall back on hope and a positive attitude. We might even be addicted to *hopium*, an irrational and unwarranted sense of optimism in the face of genuine challenge.

In this stage, we're committed to convention and are quick to trust established institutions, norms, and ideas. In this state, human life is lived in accord with standard cultural narratives and dominant myths of individualism, progress, capitalism, and human supremacy. Likewise, we're likely to subscribe to the plastic, consumeristic narratives that tell us what to buy, what to value, and how to live. We're content with the front story of modern culture and aren't much inclined to ask about the back story of our various practices, products, values, or institutions.

This condition might persist for years or even decades, but we're eventually forced into an encounter with the nasty, inconvenient, ecosocial truths of the modern world. The cold shower of scientific reality shocks us, and little by little, our comforting assumptions and beliefs begin to fall away. The realization may come as a traumatic insight, or it might come to roost as a slow, grinding pressure that squeezes the illusions out of our lives and leaves us stranded—a water torture of bad news and scientific reports, dripping on our heads, pounding the point home.

Exposure to these highly inconvenient facts, punctuated by more frequent tragedies—epic wildfires, droughts, extreme floods, and hurricanes—leads us to the dawning realization that our predicament is coming home to roost. Yes, the climate crisis is real. Yes, the biodiversity crisis is real. Yes, the scientists have been telling the truth all along. Modern civilization really is destroying its life-support system. And so, the cognitive dissonance screams: we like to think of ourselves as good people, but now it's starting to look like we are co-perpetrators in one of the most violent acts in history—the destruction of our future and the lives of our descendants.

STAGE 2: WASF

Over and over, we push the facts aside, but eventually come to accept the fact that disaster is baked into the system. We come begin to see the culture and belief system that we grew up with as not only dysfunctional, but horrifically destructive. We squirm, deny, distract, and try to run, but eventually we resign ourselves to the conclusion that *We Are So Fucked*—in short, "*WASF*".

In turn, this sucks us into a quagmire of resignation, cynicism, despair, and depression. It saps our energy and renders us inactive, immobile, and ineffective. *What exactly are we supposed to do now?* No one ever taught us anything about any of this. And so, left without apparent options, we contract and shrink back into whatever coping mechanisms we might have developed along the way. A grim sense of futurelessness dominates our experience and our spirits. We try to keep up a good front, but deep down, we're hanging on by our fingernails.

This WASF quagmire can last a very long time: years, even decades. For some, it becomes a chronic psycho-spiritual state, even a medical condition. We self-medicate, seek out therapy, distract ourselves, rationalize, and practice dark humor, but we remain mired in misery. Lost in our predicament, we try to bootstrap our way back to functionality, and maybe even some kind of happiness, but the darkness feels relentless.

This WASF stage is excruciating and even debilitating. It gums up our lives and sucks the meaning out of everything we do. But as bad as it feels, there are two important insights here and, surprisingly, some good news.

First, it's essential to remember that even though you're feeling broken, depressed, or overcome with grief, *you are not diseased.* Your body is responding the way any animal would respond to an alien, massively stressful environment. In all likelihood, there's nothing wrong with your nervous system, your brain, your body, your personality, or your spiritual life. Given the extremity of today's circumstances, your experience is to be expected. You're an animal living in highly abnormal and traumatic conditions; of course you're feeling alienated and ill at ease.

Second, the very fact that you're feeling challenged, confused, and anxious is a sign that you're paying attention to the world. The aperture of your consciousness is open far enough to let reality in. You're not in denial. You're willing to look the world in the face, listen to experts, and absorb the facts. Of course you want some peace and equanimity in your life, but for the time being, consider your suffering as a paradoxically positive marker, a sign of your consciousness and your willingness to engage. Bad as it feels right now, you may well be on the right path.

STAGE 3: WE ARE SO FOCUSED

If you're like most curious, literate people in the modern world, you've probably got at least one foot in the WASF quagmire right now. You may not be immobilized by depression, despair, or panic, but you can feel the rising anxiety, stress, and sense of urgency. The planet is always out there now, wearing down your defenses one bad headline at a time.

Fortunately, there is a way forward, a path that's being led by courageous activists around the world. Thousands of people feel the same way you do and have found a way to relevance, engagement, and meaning. These people feel the pain acutely and understand full well the depth and magnitude of our predicament. Nevertheless, they carry on, oftentimes with a powerful sense of resolve, determination, and clarity of purpose.

In this phase, we reframe our predicament from *We Are So Fucked* to *We Are So Focused*. We understand the magnitude of the challenge before us and use that extremity to power our action. There are no illusions here. Our predicament remains dire, but we find a way to get out of bed in the morning. We understand that action is the antidote to despair, and we resolve to keep fighting, no matter the outcome. We accept the exposure and risk that comes with standing up. In the process, we become increasingly proactive and courageous. We understand that the odds against success are great, but none of that matters because we're focused on the importance of our work, the creativity of our allies, and our passion for the journey.

THE ENEMY IS NEVER WRONG

This is a book about engagement, relevance, and adaptability. It's about focused, creative action in the face of epic, planet-scale ambiguity and individual stress. It offers a practical way to navigate the chaos, alienation, and fear that's rising like the very oceans around us.

Just to be clear, this is not a book about the traditional martial arts or personal self-defense. It's not about karate, aikido, or judo. Rather, this is a book about what we might call "big martial art," or what some traditional martial art teachers call "your practice off the mat."

In other words, this is a multidisciplinary look at the human experience in a conflicted world. It's about personal relationships, teaching, coaching, and politics. It's about any form of human relationship that involves conflict, which is to say, all of it. It's about navigating today's predicament with greater skill, grace, and intelligent action. It will challenge you to think clearly about the conflict in your life and, in particular, the conflict that's inherent in our attempt to create a functional future.

To put it another way, this book is about both *outward* and *inward* forms of activism. Just like it sounds, outward activism is external and includes any actions directed at the so-called outside world: filing lawsuits, protesting, performing acts of civil disobedience, and the like. Inward activism includes changes we make to our values, perspectives, ideas, attitude, and spirit. As you'll see, these forms can work together to form create a cohesive and more powerful whole.

The beauty of activism is that it puts us into a positive feedback cycle of engagement and self-discovery. Every encounter teaches us something about how the world works, also about who we are, and how we react to pressure. In this sense, activism is an essential and powerful form of education. Throw your body up against the world, and you're bound to gain important insights into your values, inclinations, prejudices, and beliefs.

When we commit to activism, everything we do takes on greater significance. What we eat, how we get from place to place, the things we buy, how we communicate, and how we relate—everything we do has consequences for how the future will unfold. In a radically interconnected world on the brink of disaster, there are no more neutral behaviors, no more ordinary moments. In the battle for the future, everything matters.

On the face of it, this may well feel like a burden—and we might even feel that the fate of the world hangs on every decision that we make each day. But this sense of responsibility is also powerfully beneficial because it concentrates our attention and keeps us focused. Engagement becomes food for our spirits and even our bodies. Once we go towards the fight, everything becomes increasingly consequential, significant, and meaningful. Participation gives us power.

Ultimately, this book won't give you a fail-safe path to effectiveness in the face of radical challenge, but it may well serve as an antidote to your feelings of despair, fatalism, depression, and apathy. To be sure, none of this is easy. No matter the depth of our skills and understanding, there will always be struggle and suffering along the way. But smart engagement will reinforce your sense of meaning and relevance. It'll put you into a virtuous circle of participation and give you some fresh ideas about strategy, behavior, and attitude. It might even change the way you touch the world.

As for our title, it comes from the traditional martial arts, where teachers sometimes advise their students that "the enemy is never wrong." This counsel may well sound preposterous on the face of it, but the lesson is both sound and relevant to the challenges of our age. The idea is to remain fluid and adaptable—don't get wrapped up in some expectation about what your situation should or shouldn't be. Your adversary, your opponent, your predicament just *is*. Abandon your psychic resistance, at least for the moment. Observe reality and adapt accordingly. Fight for what you believe in, but don't get caught up in unnecessary judgment and evaluation. Don't be trapped by your own mind.

This is not to say we should simply accept everything about the world as it is. Of course the destruction of our biosphere is wrong and must be opposed. Of course the exploitation and domination of other people is wrong and must be called out. Of course war, trauma, racism, hatred, and ignorance are wrong. Rather, this is an argument for adaptability and radical realism. It's about letting go of expectation and working with the world as it presents itself.

When we adopt this point of view, the fight remains essential, but the indignation, anxiety, and stress become optional, or at least less tyrannical. You may still struggle and suffer, but you'll see things more clearly. Your experience and your effectiveness will improve substantially. In the long run, "the enemy is never wrong" might well be the ultimate koan for stress relief, resilience, and adaptive psychology.

LIFE LESSONS

As you'll see, this book offers a series of lessons, each of which might be offered by a martial art sensei or teacher. Imagine a wise, older person who's trained hard, seen the world from different perspectives, and studied the ways of conflict, fighting, and resistance. Naturally, we'll start with fundamentals, but in fact, all these elements speak to one another, so you can read them in any order you like.

At first, you'll be wearing the white belt, a symbol of your beginner's mind, enthusiasm, and naivete. But with engagement and focused training, your belt will get dirtier and dirtier with your hard-won knowledge and experience. You may or may not become a master, but you'll be you're sure to find some focus and clarity along the way.

LESSONS

From this moment despair ends and tactics begin.

street artist Banksy

ORIENTATION

You are what you do, not what you say you'll do.

Carl Jung

You're here because you want to make a difference and you're ready to engage. You're willing to fight for what you believe in, and you want to be effective. You might even be inclined to call yourself an *activist*.

But what exactly does that mean? It's something of a new word after all, and open to some interpretation. In decades gone by, not many people described themselves in such terms, but today we hear the word applied to all kinds of people, with a wide range of values and objectives. But despite the word's increasing popularity, a solid definition remains elusive. There's no historical consensus or regulating authority that might accept or reject our language. People can use the word however they like.

In most circles, activism is seen as an activity that lies outside of normal, conventional life. It's an unusual avocation or passion, a supplement to the hard-core demands of "making a living." According to convention, it's not something that people normally do. But this view is outdated, and it's no longer good enough to think of activism as a hobby or an alternative lifestyle. Rather, activism has now become an absolutely essential element in leading a relevant, meaningful, healthy, and successful life.

But questions remain: What values does the activist

hold? How does he or she navigate the world? What's the job description? These are tricky questions because everyone engages the world in different ways, and all of us have unique situations, histories, educations, and skill sets. Everyone has their own pet issues and their own strategies for creating change. In this sense, there are probably millions of ways to be an activist, as many paths as there are people.

Most of us would agree that activism is about trying to make a difference, but at its heart, activism is a psycho-spiritual orientation, an attitude, and a perspective. Above all, it welcomes responsibility and embraces risk. It's a statement of intent, resolve, and determination, animated by discontent, a revolutionary spirit, and the belief that things could be better. And it's far more than a sideline for occasional discontent or grievance; it's a fundamental obligation for living a fully human life. As the writer Alice Walker put it, "Activism is the rent I pay for living on this planet."

THE PERILS OF INACTIVISM

In the popular imagination, it's common to think of the an activist as someone who's pushing a particular agenda. He's out there protesting, advocating, bucking the system, and trying to make a difference. But superficial appearances don't really tell us much about the content of a person's character or their relationship to life in general. What's really important is the activist's willingness, even eagerness, to pursue a life of relevance.

In this light, behaviors that sometimes masquerade as activism often don't live up to the name. It's easy to call yourself an activist, but labels are not enough. There's got to be risk, authentic engagement, and, above all, exposure. In other words, simply having an ideology, opinion, or point of view is not enough. Buying green products or an electric car is not activism. Clicking the "like" button on social media is not activism. Recycling is not activism. "Thoughts and prayers" are not activism. Complaining and worrying is not activism. Being a fan of other people's activism is not activism.

In essence, these are superficial forms of armchair activism, or to put it another way, *inactivism*. There's no real risk or exposure here, no embrace of responsibility, no real intention to act. The inactivist hides out in convention, safely insulated from the perils of genuine engagement. If challenged, he evades and justifies: *It's not my job.* He follows the standard cultural script and the doctrine of convenience, which is to say, he takes the path well-traveled. Stay positive, go along, keep your head down, stay close to the status quo, and, above all, don't rock the lifeboat, even when the water's pouring in. And when the stress hits the fan, revert to the familiar—familiar activities, ideas, and culture. That's where the safety is.

THE ACTIVIST ORIENTATION

In contrast, the activist has a distinctive set of qualities and a certain kind of character. In particular, he embraces an obligation to act, especially if he's fortunate enough to have some advantages in life. When challenged, he takes it on: *It is my job.* Activists are willing—even eager—to accept exposure and risk and to venture outside their familiar physical, social, and cultural comfort zones. They're willing—even eager—to disrupt conventional culture by standing up, speaking out, blowing the whistle, or taking a knee. They're prepared to accept risk, not for just for stimulation or amusement, but intentionally, for a purpose. In short, the activist is a stand-up animal.

This orientation extends deep into the activist's life and his or her relationship with the world. Not only do they embrace the big-picture challenges that affect the entire planet, society, and culture, they also take responsibility for the little things they encounter each day. In this sense, activism isn't just about spectacular acts of protest and charismatic battles with monstrous forces of darkness; it's also about the way we treat the world and each other in ordinary encounters. To put it another way, activism is about much more than political protest and civil disobedience; it's about how we choose to live, even when no one is watching.

OUT OF THE DARKNESS

The activist may have a compelling interest in a certain problem, crisis, or injustice, but the orientation goes far beyond the details of any particular issue. Activists are seekers, hungry for understanding and determined to get to the heart of reality. They refuse to be content with easy, superficial explanations about how the world works, and they're vigilant in calling out deception, misinformation, and falsehood.

Above all, the activist is determined to tell the truth. This radical honesty is a core psycho-spiritual quality of all activism, no matter the domain or issue, and in this respect, activists and scientists are natural allies. Scientists are honor-bound to integrity in their methods, data, and the reporting of their results. In the scientific community, there is no greater sin than dishonesty. Error is acceptable—even productive—but truth must be paramount.

Likewise, the activist is willing—even eager—to look reality in the face, no matter how revolting, disturbing, or frustrating that view might be. As a passenger on lifeboat Earth, the activist sees the gaping hole in the hull, sees the people chopping away to make it bigger, sees the water pouring in, and gets to work. There's no evasion of responsibility, no denial, and no attempt to feel better about it. To put it another way, the activist is someone who's awake to the world and his or her place in it. Some observers say that humanity is "sleepwalking into an age of extinction," but activists refuse to join in the denial and delusion. They're prepared to see the world as it is, without wishful thinking or hope.

In this way, the activist is very much like the philosopher of Plato's cave. As you might remember, Plato was a Greek philosopher who imagined a group of people living in a dark cave, watching as the light from a fire cast flickering shapes upon the wall. By appearance, the shadows seem to reveal the nature of the world, but this is nothing more than illusion. The philosopher and the activist are people who've escaped the cave and discovered the true—and sometimes disturbing—nature of reality on the outside.

Plato's allegory is a perfect metaphor for the digital addiction of our time, but it also implies a job description for the activist—pulling people out of the darkness, into the light of the real world. In this sense, we might well say that the activist is a teacher, a coach, a leader, and even an attentional therapist—someone who helps others see the world in new, and more accurate ways.

REMEMBER THIS...

All of which puts our predicament into sharp relief and presents us with a challenge. Will you shrink back into the comfort, safety, and irrelevance of inactivism and the false images projected on the walls of your digital cave? Or will you embrace the responsibility, the risk, and the vulnerability that comes with engagement? You're just one person, and maybe you feel powerless in the face of such massive challenges, but the process begins here, now. Engagement is intimidating, but it will also make you stronger. Ultimately, relevance is the path forward.

INQUIRY

Victorious warriors win first and then go to war,
while defeated warriors go to war first and then
seek to win.

Sun Tzu

The Art of War

For the beginner, impulsive action comes naturally. We feel threatened, frightened, or distressed, and our bodies take over. Hearts pounding, blood pressure rising, stress hormones surging, we lash out, freeze up, or flee the scene. It's easy to get emotional, and, given the perilous state of the modern world, it's perfectly understandable. We're whipsawed by events, each one seemingly more vital and consequential than the last. We feel the need to act, and the sooner the better, but impulse is notoriously counterproductive and mostly serves to plunge us deeper into conflict, anger, confusion, and ineffectiveness. That's why it's a good idea to ask some foundational questions about our ultimate objectives. As Socrates might have put it, "*The unexamined fight is not worth fighting.*" Reactivity, we might say, is the real enemy.

BIG INQUIRY

Sadly, this is where so many of us go wildly wrong. Without an inquiry, you'll stumble through life, and your activism will be weak and erratic. The power of questions and objectives is that they keep us focused, help us avoid the distraction of petty squabbles, and preserve our energy for what really matters. For the martial artist, it's a practical matter; when you stop asking questions, you become vulnerable to surprise attack and all manner of calamity. But even more importantly, inquiry is also a crucial marker of health and wildness; when the human animal is healthy, the sense of wonder and curiosity flows naturally.

The challenge is to sustain our sense of wonder and to view the world with beginner's eyes, as if for the first time, even in the face of massively inconvenient truths. Can you relinquish your hold on your cherished assumptions and static, finite knowledge? Can you wake up to the familiar qualities of experience and question the "obvious" qualities of your life?

Ideally, we'd question everything in our experience, but for the activist, there are essential questions that must be asked in advance, before engagement begins:

Question your predicament. What kind of problem is this? Is it technological? Political? Cultural? Relational? Frame the predicament in the right way, and your action will be effective; frame it wrong, and you're going to get into trouble.

Question the history. How did this situation come to be? The forces of history are immensely powerful in shaping behavior and outcomes. Knowing the arc of history will tell you about trends, trajectories, and leverage points.

Question your education and training. What was I taught and why? What circumstance was I being prepared for? What are the underlying values that drove my schooling?

Was the process even relevant to the world I am about to inhabit?

Question the terrain. What domain am I operating in? What are the power relationships? Who makes the decisions? What are the rules and expectations? Is change possible? If so, how?

Question the human animal. What kind of history do humans share? How do we typically behave? Are we rational actors, or are we fundamentally impulsive? What are our typical needs? What do we typically attach to and identify with?

Question your adversaries. What do they value? What are their interests and positions? What kind of power do they wield? What motivates them? What are their objectives?

Question your culture. What are the core assumptions and values of my culture? What are the rituals and beliefs? Is it a new culture, or does it have a long tradition? Is my culture static, or is it open to change? How does it behave in the face of challenge and conflict?

Question your sources. Where does my information come from? Are my facts reliable? Are they cross-checked against other standards of knowledge? Or are they simply pumped into my brain via a customized digital feed?

Question your motives. What moves me? What drives my behavior? What makes me feel safe? What gives me a sense of satisfaction and meaning? How do I behave when under stress? What am I trying to create?

BIG OBJECTIVES

For every aspiring activist, an essential first step is to question our ultimate goals and objectives. What am I trying to achieve? What's my target? What's my reference point for action? How will I know if I'm on the right path?

Naturally, everyone will have their own favorite issues and interests, but ultimately, the thing that really matters is the viability of the biosphere. Without question, the planet is the elephant in the room and the alpha issue of our age. Everything we might ever want depends on this. When your lifeboat has a hole in it and the water is gushing in, all other issues become secondary. As the writer Naomi Klein has put it, "When your life support system is threatened, all other problems fit inside that problem."

Naturally, many of us are drawn to a "save the world" narrative. We can all agree that it's a worthy goal, but on the other hand, it might be too vague and ambitious to be helpful. But even more problematic is the language. "Saving the world" suggests that we—*Homo sapiens*—are the master of the biosphere and all life on Earth. In other words, it's more of the same anthropocentric, human-centered orientation that's caused so much trouble in the first place.

So maybe we can narrow it down to something more specific. Perhaps you'd like to "save the habitability of the planet." Maybe you'd like to "save biodiversity," "rewild the planet," or "preserve habitat." Maybe you'd like to—as conservationist Aldo Leopold famously put it—"save all the cogs and wheels." Maybe you'd like to change our culture to something more consistent with ecological reality and human needs. Or maybe you'd simply like to create a functional future, something that actually works.

Some writers suggest that the time has come to "end the fossil-fueled domination of the planet." Others say that industrial civilization has run its course, and all we can do now is work for "degrowth," a "graceful collapse," or "a radical contraction of human activity and impact." Likewise, some philosophers argue that the time has come to "abolish the doctrine of human supremacy" and "return humans to a biocentric relationship with life on earth."

Similarly, ecotheologians tell us that the supreme objective should be to develop a "right relationship with reality." Others argue that our prime directive should be to ease the suffering of people, plants, animals, and habitat around the planet. All of which aligns with what ecotheologian Thomas Berry described as "the great work," reweaving ourselves back into participation with the circle of life.

These are grand, noble objectives and they serve a valuable guiding purpose, but in order for us to be truly effective, we've got to tighten our focus and concentrate on a particular issue, a particular policy, a particular region or species. Maybe it's fossil fuels, plastics, or a certain forest, river, or grassland. Maybe it's social or economic justice, racism, women's reproductive rights, democracy, voting rights, or education.

These are all vital issues, but as you'll soon discover, even these objectives are immense and intimidating. So you'll need to narrow things down again, and again, until you arrive at something you can actually grasp. Keep getting specific until you find something that's actually doable. Will you focus on direct action against new fossil fuel projects? Which ones? Will you work on government policy and regulation? How so? Will you attempt to steer culture in a new direction with education, writing, and speaking? What will that look like? What exactly are you going to do with your precious time?

This drive for precision will make you a more effective activist, but it's also important to check back with your original, grand aspirations from time to time. Ask yourself, *Does my specific action serve my larger goal and objective? Does this current microbattle align with my larger purpose? Does it serve "the great work"?* If not, an adjustment will be in order.

FOR OR AGAINST?

At the same time, you'll want to consider a simple, foundational question: Am I fighting *for* or *against* something? The question may sound trivial or philosophical, but in fact, the answer will be extremely consequential for the way your activism plays out. The fundamental difference is this: fighting *against* is likely to be reactive and defensive; but fighting *for* is likely to be creative and energizing.

Fighting against tends to be the weaker form because its aspirations are limited; it doesn't look beyond the possibility of victory. The best that you can hope for is the preservation of some status quo. Fighting against feels protective and reactionary, and there's a good chance that it'll stimulate brain regions that fire your stress response: the famous fight-or-flight reaction of the autonomic nervous system. This adversarial focus may well be a necessary act of protection, and it may even be honorable, but it can only succeed up to a point. You may succeed in defeating or containing your adversary, but beyond your individual victory, you may not achieve or create anything of lasting value.

In contrast, fighting for is often the more powerful form

because it implies growth and creativity; there's simply more potential here. Fighting for feels meaningful and maybe even boundless. You're focused on something of value, and you want that thing to expand into the future.

This is why Native Americans have reframed their activism around pipelines and fossil-fuel projects, saying things like, "We aren't protesters; we're water protectors." It's not so much that we're fighting *against* pipelines; it's that we're fighting *for* the health and vitality of the habitat that supports our lives. In other words, we're conscientious protectors. It's a subtle but powerful shift of emphasis.

In the world of competitive sports, this contrast of between *for* and *against* is widely understood by coaches. Playing defense is a psycho-spiritual orientation that's sometimes called "being on your back foot." You aren't playing your game plan; you're merely reacting. You aren't taking the fight to your opponent; you're simply trying to contain them. When a team or individual is stuck playing defense, defeat becomes nearly inevitable.

So ask yourself:

Are you fighting *against* injustice or *for* social equality?

Are you fighting *against* habitat destruction or *for* a healthy human-habitat relationship?

Are you fighting *against* the tribe on the other side of the river, or are you fighting *for* dialogue, communication, and mutual interest?

Are you fighting *against* the corporate forces that are destroying vital habitat, or are you fighting *for* the rights of nature and an ecologically sane human culture?

Naturally, this for-or-against duality is something of an artificial simplification; in real life, the martial artist must be ambidextrous and capable of both orientations. There will be times to fight against opposing forces—and to be sure, when it comes to the biosphere, this is surely one of those times. But but don't get hyper-focused on your adversary, no matter how pathological his behavior happens to be. Save some energy for your creative work and remember what you're trying to accomplish.

REMEMBER THIS...

Curiosity is your superpower. No matter the heat and stress of your engagement with the world, keep your inquiry alive. Take charge of the process by asking questions, not just about the action of the day, but as a sustained, life-long lifelong discipline and practice.

Success will come when you take the time to pause and reflect, again and again. Go back up on the mountain and renew your vision. Work with a coach, a teacher, or an elder to refine your objectives. Write them down or discuss them with others. Your vision may change, and you'll probably have to revise your path along the way, but without a point of focus, you'll wander the landscape, waste your energy, and fail as an activist. Instead, pick an issue, refine it, and take it as far as you can.

LIFE SUPPORT

I live my life in widening circles that reach out
across the world.

Rainer Maria Rilke

If you want to succeed as a martial artist, or even make a go of it as a functional human being, you had better know something about what keeps you alive. *What are the systems and processes that sustain me? What nourishes my life? What gives me my wildness, my health, and my vitality?* This understanding will be essential in guiding your activism and giving you a sense of focus; it'll tell you what you're fighting for.

In our original hunter-gatherer world of the Paleolithic era, there was never much confusion about any of this. People were fully immersed in habitat and constantly reminded of life-supporting realities. But today, the artificial world lulls us into ignorance and denial with comforting layers of insulation and convenience. In this kind of environment, it's easy to forget the fundamentals.

Consequently, many people in the modern world are living in a profound state of ignorance. Many of us have no real idea where our food comes from; it's not just children who believe that food and water come from the store or is brought to our table by a server. And with our senses constantly bombarded by digital stimulation, distraction has become the default state for much of humanity. Literally and psycho-spiritually, most of us are completely out of touch with what keeps us alive.

Fortunately, it's pretty easy to understand the basics. Modern science, coupled with indigenous understanding, shows us three distinct circles of life support that surround the human body: *habitat, people,* and *story*—especially the cultural narratives that give our lives meaning and direction. From a biological and psycho-social point of view, these three circles make sense—and in a fundamental way, they're all that humans really need.

HABITAT

Not only does habitat gives us our food, water, and air, it also gives us beauty and a sense of wonder, identity and even sanity. It's no surprise that native and indigenous people have long felt a powerful sense of continuity with habitat, often expressed in the declaration "I am the land, the land is me." This level of life support has been foundational for humans throughout history, and it's only in the last few hundred years that people have come to the historically abnormal conclusion that human life is somehow possible independent of habitat.

In fact, many modern people have no meaningful relationship whatsoever with their local habitat. If you live in an urban setting, you might not even see, much less touch, your local natural world. And even worse, much of our behavior toward the habitat around us is violent and massively self-defeating. None of this is remotely sustainable; destroy your habitat and you destroy yourself.

TRIBE AND COMMUNITY

The next circle of life-support life support is made of people. As hypersocial animals, we are radically dependent on our relationships with others, and it's no exaggeration to describe these connections as life sustaining. A vast body of research in social psychology and interpersonal neurobiology tells us that human community is essential for our survival and function. As social neuroscientists sometimes put it, "The brain is a social organ." Our deep-seated need for social affiliation is so strong that, in effect, "There are no single human brains."

Likewise, research points to the power of social attachment in promoting health, happiness, and success in life. People who form secure attachments to caregivers in childhood are far more likely to thrive in adulthood. In fact, the quality of this attachment turns out to be a better predictor of success than conventional measures such as IQ and test scores. In short, strong relationships make us healthier and, in all likelihood, more effective as activists.

Not surprisingly, our Paleolithic ancestors were quick to recognize the life-supporting power of society and tribe. Life in a wild, predator-rich environment was dangerous and demanded that people circle up and stay together. As a result, humans had a compelling interest in matters of acceptance and rejection, inclusion and exclusion. To be accepted was to be safe, but to be banished was something very close to a death sentence.

This prosocial identification shows up in many indigenous and Eastern cultures but is most conspicuous in the African social philosophy of *ubuntu* (pronounced uu-boon-too). According to ubuntu, there exists a common bond between all human beings, and it is through this bond that we discover our own human qualities; we affirm our humanity when we acknowledge the humanity of others. To be is to be a part of the group.

In other words, native people tend to define themselves primarily as participants in a larger social order. As the bushmen of South Africa put it, "We are people through other people," and "I am what I am because of who we are." Or, as Archbishop Desmond Tutu put it, "You can't be human on your own." This theme is common, if not universal, among indigenous peoples, but tragically, this sense of social identification has largely broken down and has been replaced by a growing sense of xenophobia, individualism, ambition, and narcissism—a new asocial orientation that *New York Times* columnist David Brooks calls "the Big Me."

So perhaps it's not surprising that we see such striking levels of social dysfunction, friction, and outright alienation in today's world. There's plenty of talk about polarization, and in the United States, a "cold civil war," but that's just the beginning. Our original tribal bands have been replaced by vast, impersonal networks that connect us superficially but fail to sustain. Authentic conversation, once a mainstay of daily interaction, has been replaced by automated, scripted, plastic forms of transaction.

STORY

The third circle of life support is composed of meaning, narrative, and culture. This is what tells us about our place in the world and, above all, gives us a sense of purpose. Without this influence, we'd be lost, confused, and maybe even terrified.

In the lives of our prehistoric hunting-and-gathering ancestors, story and culture served their purpose well. People gathered around the campfire at night and listened to the elders speak. We can be certain that some of their stories were funny, some sad, and some profound, but taken together, these narratives provided an explanation—a unified understanding of life and, in particular, human relationships with the natural world. Common themes of interdependence, animism, and permeability were woven throughout these tellings and helped people experience a unity with nature.

But today we lack this kind of unifying narrative. We're surrounded by millions of stories, but most are told with ulterior motives. They tell us what to buy and what kind of lifestyle to live, but rarely do they provide any kind of relational guidance or insight into our place in the cosmos. To put it another way, we're suffering a crisis of meaning. We don't know what we're striving for or which direction we're headed. Are we headed back to some kind of primal, back-to-the-land experience, or are we surging forward to a high-tech utopia? No one seems to know. It's no wonder we're so anxious.

FAUX LIFE SUPPORT

These circles of life support might well seem obvious, but, sadly, a substantial number of people have come to believe that our primary life-support circle is something called *the economy*. If this system is deemed healthy, then all is well and we have nothing to worry about. This is why we're constantly updated with diagnostic indicators of economic vitality: stock market performance, gross domestic product, jobs reports, and other measures. If the economy is okay, all is well—so the story goes.

But this belief is ultimately distracting and even delusional. It ignores the reality of our primal life-giving systems, and replaces it with a vast system of artificial incentives and market forces. In the process, it radically distorts traditional human attention, social relations, and values. In the modern age, we have become a for-profit society, with a for-profit culture, powered by a for-profit value system. People and living systems are treated like disposable externalities that can safely be ignored. Nature is simply a department store, and the future is little more than a sacrifice zone.

On the face of it, economists might seem to have a point—on an immediate, practical level, we do have to pay the rent and "put food on the table." But from a big history point of view, economic systems are actually a recent, novel, and largely untested innovations. For the vast majority of our time on earth, humans have lived without any kind of economic calculation or transactions whatsoever. To be sure, people have always traded, but it would be a mistake to say that an economy is absolutely essential to human survival. Money only appeared in human civilization a few thousand years ago. In other words, we have a proven ability to survive without it.

The problem with money is that it lulls us into false beliefs about what really matters and what might be possible. In daily life, money solves all sorts of practical problems, and before long, many of us come to think of it as omnipotent. Money can rescue us from almost any predicament and cure our anxiety—so it appears. And so we strive incessantly: *"If I can get enough of a cushion, I'll be protected from uncertainty, and I'll be safe."*

But in reality, this thing we call the economy is utterly dependent on a healthy biosphere. There is no work-around or technological fix. If ecosystems fail, the economy fails. As the various internet memes put it: *There is no economy on a dead planet. There are no jobs on a dead planet. There is no profit on a dead planet.* Or as climate scientist Guy McPherson puts it, "If you think the economy is more important than the environment, try holding your breath while counting your money."

In other words, the economy is not a true life-support system. On the contrary, research demonstrates that money can be a profoundly disruptive, anti-tribal, even anti-human force. In her research at the University of Minnesota, Kathleen Vohs primed subjects with reminders of economics, finance, prices, and costs, and discovered that

> . . . money-primed people behave more selfishly and show a greater reluctance to be involved

with others… Even in intimate relationships and collectivistic cultures, reminders of money weaken sociomoral responses.

These findings, described by the Nobel Prize winner Daniel Kahneman in *Thinking, Fast and Slow*, are profoundly inconvenient to culture-as-usual. Obviously, people who live in the modern world are massively and continuously "money-primed." Immersed in a world of twenty-four-hour commerce, advertising, special offers, and discount pricing, we're reminded of money hundreds of times each day. If these priming events incline us even slightly away from our historically normal pro-tribal, prosocial orientations, the overall effect is destructive on a planetary scale. In effect, money is a corrosive agent, an acid that dissolves normal human communities.

REWEAVE

The beauty of our new-old understanding of life-support is that it gives us a value system, a sense of priority, and even some ethical guidance. It also helps us navigate the complexity and practical confusions that we often face. With so many competing demands for attention and action, it's hard to know what to do when we get up in the morning. *What battles shall I fight today? Shall I work for energy efficiency, social justice, health care, habitat preservation, media hygiene, or just try to keep my head above water?* It's no wonder that so many of us feel overcome by complexity and confusion.

Perhaps a re-orientation will help. In his great classic, *A Sand County Almanac*, conservationist Aldo Leopold described a "land ethic" that can give us guidance: "A thing is right when it tends to preserve the integrity, stability, and beauty of the biotic community. It is wrong when it tends otherwise."

Well said, but we might expand our thinking to include everything that sustains us: "*A thing is right when it tends to preserve the integrity, stability, and beauty of our life-supporting systems of habitat, community, and meaning. It is wrong when it tends otherwise.*"

This understanding simplifies our action and gives us focus. As long as our activism engages one of the three life-supporting circles, we're doing something right. When chaos and complexity surge, pick one of the circles and dig in:

Begin with the body. There's massive suffering at this level and plenty of opportunity to make a difference. Help people feel better in their bodies, and they're more likely to make a meaningful contribution. Any work you do in the domain of health promotion, vitality, and medicine is going to go a long way.

Work at the level of habitat. Become an advocate for preservation, conservation, and rewilding. Remind people of the soil, water, plants, and animals that keep them alive. Show them the beauty and power of nature, and tell them what happens when ecosystems become impoverished through exploitation and fragmentation. Become a champion for biodiversity.

Work at the level of people and society. Become involved with community development, therapy, coaching, or leadership. Facilitate conversation in safe environments. Teach language and the humanities. Connect people to one another with authentic experience. Give them the opportunity to metabolize their trauma and grow into new relationships.

Work at the level of story and culture. Write, produce, direct; help us find some kind of unifying narrative that will illuminate our path and give us a sense of meaning and purpose. Speak a truth that will light our way to a functional future.

STAND WITH THE CIRCLES...

Once again, this is where the activist serves a crucial function as a leader and attentional coach. As you engage, remind people what really keeps them alive. When they drift back into distraction and confusion, redirect them to the circles. And above all, nurture what nurtures you. When conditions get confusing or chaotic, don't despair. Circle back to the circles, and you won't go far wrong.

ENGAGEMENT

Opportunities multiply as they are seized.

Sun Tzu

The Art of War

The time has come to step up and act. You've done your homework and studied your alpha issue. You know something about your adversaries and their relationships, their philosophies, histories, and powers. You may not have much experience and you're right to feel challenged, even intimidated, but there can be no backing out now. You're committed. But before you choose a specific course of action, you'll want to give some thought to what's moving you.

FEEL GOOD OR DO GOOD?

Begin with this simple question. Are you simply trying simply to ease your anxiety and satisfy an urge for destruction? Or are you trying to move the needle on how the world actually works? These questions demand reflection and force us to consider our deeper motivations. You may not have thought about your activism in these terms, but this is a pivotal inquiry that can guide you through all kinds of uncertainty and turmoil, for the rest of your life.

When the stakes and tensions are high, it's natural to want a quick resolution. When people and corporations are destroying habitat, taking away human rights, or compromising everyone's future, you're right to feel hurt, angry, or traumatized. The feeling is toxic and corrosive, and calls for action. We want to bring the perpetrators to a grinding halt, stop them in their tracks, destroy their machines, constrain their power, cripple their financial power, and maybe even make them suffer. Then we might at least *feel* better.

But feeling good is not the same thing as making real changes that effectively stop the destruction in the long run. It might *feel* good to vandalize a bulldozer, but it really stop deforestation on a large scale? It might *feel* good to riot in the streets, but will that really stop widespread racism or police brutality? It might *feel* good to deflate the tires on climate-destroying SUVs, but will that really turn the tide of atmospheric catastrophe?

To be sure, there's something to be said for the human need for expression, and sometimes we simply want to make a statement regardless of whether it has any palpable or systemic impact. But if we're going to create meaningful, substantive transformation, we've got to keep our emotions in check, at least for the moment. In other words, *doing good must be the first priority; feeling good can wait.*

And so, we redouble our efforts and focus on the systems, methods, policies, and values that sustain our adversaries and their destructive practices. Go to the heart, go to the root, and find the origins of whatever it is you're taking on. Work on changing the laws, policies, and cultural beliefs that drive the devastation. And, if you can succeed in this effort, even in some small measure, you're going to feel really good in the long run.

INSIDE OR OUTSIDE?

Another pivotal question for aspiring activists has to do with your position in relationship to the system in question. As conventional wisdom has it, being outside the halls of power leaves you helpless, but being inside gives you the chance to make real, if incremental, change. Once you're inside, you'll know the rules, the people, and the culture, and you'll be in a position to exercise some influence. Or, maybe you can act as a covert operative and subvert the system from within.

But contrarians argue that all of this is unlikely. Once you're inside some big system, you're almost certainly going to be swallowed up in the prevailing culture and value system. Social influence is powerful, and groupthink is common in large organizations. It takes a lot of fortitude to work inside a system and maintain your original values and perspective.

This argues for staying *outside* and working externally. In theory, this position gives you an independent perspective and objectivity that will help you stay focused on your goals. The problem, of course, is that when you're outside, you're unlikely to have much leverage. Most modern organizations and systems are highly insulated: physically, socially, and legally. Some are nearly impenetrable and impervious to public input and opinion. You can bang on the door with lawsuits, petitions, and demands, but you may not get anywhere at all.

The dilemma sounds intractable, but there is a third way: *all of the above.* Take a stand wherever you are and work with whatever power and influence you've got. If you're inside, tweak existing policies and procedures as best you can. Challenge bad practices and propose better ones. Look for slack in the system and make it work for you. If you're outside, challenge destructive systems with law, narrative, culture, and civil disobedience. Call attention to the bad practices that are taking place inside the walls. You may not be able to challenge the existing system directly, but the simple act of shining the light is potentially powerful.

Above all, look for alliances that cross the walls: If you're outside, talk to people on the inside. Find out how their systems work, what they're doing, and what they value. What's their culture? What are the leverage points for change? If you're on the inside, talk to people on the outside for new ideas and energy. Maybe there are some work-arounds that you're not seeing. Take your leverage where you can find it. No system is completely impervious to influence.

UPSTREAM OR DOWNSTREAM?

To be effective, you'll also want to consider your position in relation to the flow of history and events. Will you be working downstream to put out the fires of consequence and bad planning? Or will you fight upstream, at the root of the problem? You may not always have a choice in the matter, but asking the question will go a long ways towards making a difference.

Naturally, upstream action is likely to be far more consequential in the long run. If you can get to the origins of the crisis in question, you've got a chance to prevent all manner of downstream chaos. As Archbishop Desmond Tutu put it, "We need to stop just pulling people out of the river. We need to go upstream and find out why they're falling in." To put it another way, an ounce of upstream work is worth a ton of downstream desperation. Or, as a Native American saying has it, "It's easier to build strong children than to repair broken men."

Sadly, modern culture is often pointed in the wrong direction on this score. Upstream solutions lack the prestige and dramatic appeal of downstream heroics. And to make matters worse, a host of perverse economic incentives give us a systemic bias against acting early. We pay big money for downstream "solutions," but we pay almost nothing to people operating at the root of our various afflictions.

Examples abound: We promote downstream carbon capture instead of preventing carbon emissions at their source. We give attention to downstream plastic cleanup instead of making upstream reductions in plastic production. We promote downstream tree-planting instead of upstream limits on deforestation. We lionize downstream medical heroics instead of upstream prevention and public health. We pay vast sums to incarcerate people in prisons, but pay little to the health, educational, and social workers who keep people whole and functional in the first place. All of which leaves us in a perpetual state of panic, constantly cleaning up the messes left to us by yesterday's shortsighted decision makers.

Wisdom suggests that we adopt an aggressive upstream orientation, aimed specifically and explicitly at the prevention of downstream problems. And it all begins with inquiry: What's the history of the issue in question? How did this ugly outcome come to be? Where was the upstream leverage point for today's catastrophe? And how can we get to the source of the issue in question?

Most obviously, we need to rewire the perverse incentives that drive people away from upstream action, but even more to the point, we need a radical reorientation towards origins in general. The word "radical" is often assumed to mean something outside the bounds of convention—something extreme, disruptive, and even destructive. But in fact, the word is from the Latin *radicalis*, *radix*, *radic*—meaning "root." In other words, the radical is someone who's trying to get to the ultimate origin of the problem. And, in this sense, radicalism is actually the essence of intelligent action. Acting at the root is not only more likely to be effective, it's profoundly pro-health and pro-future. Get in on the action early, and you can make some meaningful change.

A RADICAL ANIMAL

All of which may well seem like an impossible challenge. You'd like to work upstream, but in today's culture, you probably won't be getting much support or reward for your efforts. And to make matters even more challenging, you might not see the results of your work for years, decades, or maybe not even in your lifetime.

But you are far from powerless. In fact, the simple act of moving your attention upstream makes you a thousand times more powerful in the long run. Small, seemingly trivial actions at the root will have big consequences down the line. You may not *feel* powerful, but your work is making a real downstream difference.

As an activist, your job is to keep people focused on the upstream origins of wicked problems. Once again, think of yourself as an attentional coach, reminding people that today's problems have a history and that acting early is the wisest approach.

This orientation also changes the way we view our actions in the moment. You may not be able to travel back in time and fix the dysfunctions at their source, but from another perspective, you're already living at the point of origin. Realize it or not, you're always living upstream. To put it another way, today is always upstream of tomorrow.

CULTURE JAM

The first step—especially for young people with energy and drive and talent, but not money—the first step to controlling your world is to control your culture. To model and demonstrate the kind of world you demand to live in. To write the books. Make the music. Shoot the films. Paint the art.

Novelist Chuck Palahniuk

When going into battle, it hardly needs to be said that it's wise to identify your adversary with precision: the who or what you're fighting against. Otherwise, you're going to waste a lot of energy, gum up the works, and make yourself vulnerable. And even if you somehow prevail with superior force, you might well have defeated someone or something that wasn't really a threat in the first place.

Sadly, this is how we so often behave. Forging ahead on impulse, we say that we're fighting "the bad guys." We feel anxious, insecure, and vulnerable, and we lash out. In this state, almost any target will do, and it doesn't matter much whether we get it right or not. We just want to push back against someone or something, anyone or anything. We crave the battle and the feeling of resistance. But even if we happen to prevail, this is not martial artistry. It's just frustration in action.

So we've got to get specific:

Who's the real villain in this drama?

Is my problem an individual, an organization, a policy, or a system?

Is it an idea, a group, an institution, or an attitude?

Is my issue localized, or is it embedded and distributed across large scale systems?

Is it concrete and tangible, or is it conceptual and abstract?

As we look around at the devastation of our modern life-support systems, one emerging school of thought paints our predicament with an extremely broad brush and declares *Homo sapiens* the ultimate villain. This view is expressed in a range of increasingly distressing metaphors: humanity is the disease, a virus, a pathogen, a cancer on the earth, and so on. "Get rid of humanity, and you've solved the problem," people say. In short, the enemy is us.

It's understandable and maybe even tempting to jump on this bandwagon, but it's also a path to nowhere. It assumes that the entire species is inherently flawed and that people are destined to destroy themselves. Even worse, there's nothing to be done about any of it. There's no future worth talking about and it's game over for our species and the planet. All of which pulls us right back into the quagmire of depression, cynicism, nihilism, and despair.

But this philosophy—if you can call it that—ignores the simple fact that human cultures vary dramatically and that many have lived in rough harmony with the natural world for thousands, even tens of thousands of years. In particular, native and indigenous societies have a long history of intimacy with the natural world, and, in fact, native cultures of

Africa and Australia have been some of the most successful and sustainable on earth. In other words, some humans do manage to get it right.

In contrast, modern Western culture is something of a historical outlier. Starting with the ancient Greeks, and accelerating with the scientific revolution, modern people have largely divorced themselves from the natural world in a kind of self-declared alienation. In the process, we've created a culture that's not only highly destructive to nature, it's also antithetical to sustainability and ecological sanity. If we're looking for a perpetrator and a target for our action, this would be a good place to start.

IT'S THE CULTURE, STUPID

The sad fact is that modern culture is inherently ecocidal. Not only does it glorify wealth and flagrant consumption, it also incentivizes us to exploit and ultimately destroy our life-support system. Modern culture tells us in no uncertain terms that humans are the supreme life-form on the planet and that the natural world is nothing more than a resource to be exploited. This narrative allows us to perpetrate violence against forests, oceans, habitats, species, and even future generations of our own kind. We turn communities into commodities, and relatives into resources.

Naturally, there's plenty of scholarship on how human cultures have come to be and plenty of speculation on how they work. But for the moment, we can boil it down to two prevailing attitudes about the human relationship to nature. In his book *Ishmael*, Daniel Quinn described these fundamental orientations towards the world at large: "Taker" cultures see the natural world as a resource to be exploited. "Leaver" cultures see themselves as guests on the planet. For Leavers, the natural world is seen as intrinsically valuable, completely apart from any economic value it might have for humans. This is sometimes described as a biocentric or deep ecology orientation. In this kind of culture, humans are simply one species among many, neither above nor below the rest of creation.

HOW TO FIGHT A CULTURE

So what does this mean for the martial artist and the activist? How does one fight something as vast, and embedded as a culture? It's not like hand-to-hand combat against a single adversary; culture is diffuse and entrenched, hard to grasp, and difficult to pin down. Nevertheless, there are some tactics that hold promise.

Most important is the realization that *culture is not carved in stone*. It's tempting to assume that the culture we grew up with in is the only possible option and that our role is simply to reproduce what we've been taught. This orientation is massively reinforced in school and in narratives that circulate through popular media. Living inside this belief system, it may never occur to us that culture can change; our job is simply to perpetuate what was handed to us. If we reproduce the beliefs and rituals of our youth, we've succeeded.

But in fact, culture is malleable, and most of us can have a voice in its trajectory. From this perspective, life begins to look a lot different and a lot more exciting. We aren't just reproducing what's been handed to us, we're actively constructing and defining our cultural future. For the artistic activist, culture becomes another medium, a space for our creativity to flourish.

Stories, rituals, choices, values, music, and books: it's all up for grabs. There's no law saying that you have to behave the way the people around you are behaving. You may not be as influential as a cultural celebrity with a big megaphone, but you can still make a difference in the way culture evolves. You're a creative human animal after all.

In fact, humans are actively sculpting culture in every minute of every day. Everything we do either reinforces prevailing culture or counters it: every act we perform, every decision we make, every word that we speak has some influence. We are not condemned to reproduce the culture that's been handed to us.

But how can we change our culture to be more humane and more inclusive of the natural world? How can we make it more functional and relevant to the facts of our predicament? How can we make it future-friendly?

Some of us will go straight to the heart of the matter and call out the underlying cultural attitudes, values, and narratives that lead to planet-hostile behavior. But this direct approach can be tricky. Full-frontal assaults on any human culture are likely to provoke furious resistance. Most people are strongly attached to their familiar values and rituals and are prepared to do almost anything to defend them, even when that culture is headed towards disaster. A reflexive, unconscious defense of Mother culture is probably a human universal.

So perhaps an indirect approach would be wiser. In this, we seek to broaden our adversaries' minds, not with direct assaults on their values, but by offering an expanded perspective. Coax the enemy into a new understanding of the human experience. Read about the life ways of other people and the diversity of their world views. Talk with a variety of people and share what you've learned. Many listeners will be astonished to learn that the culture of their youth is not the only way to live and view the world. When they discover that other possibilities exist, they just might soften their perspective and maybe even come around to your way of thinking.

This is why disciplines like travel, history, and anthropology are so vital. Every time we experience another world-view, we're pulled into new possibilities. Every time we teach another orientation, we invite people to reconsider their assumptions. In the process, resistance softens, and people might even come around to our way of thinking with no effort whatsoever. Call it educational martial artistry if you like; victory comes with a more expansive perspective.

CULTURAL ACTIVISM

As for specific tactics, this is a wide-open field of possibility. You may feel like an over-matched bit player up against titanic cultural forces, but modern activists have taken the fight to corporate consumerism with an exciting form of media jujitsu. Specifically, these activists have taken on big-money advertising with *subvertising* (a portmanteau of "subversive" and "advertising"), parodies, and *brandalism* (a portmanteau of "brand" and "vandalism"). They've intervened in public spaces, altering billboards, bus stop posters, and other public advertising. In the process, they use corporate messaging against itself.

In essence, this is both an anti-advertising movement and an attack on *affluenza* (a portmanteau of "affluence" and "influenza"). Writers and documentary filmmakers have defined affluenza as a kind of cultural disease, "a painful, contagious, socially transmitted condition of overload, debt, anxiety, and waste resulting from the dogged pursuit of more." Likewise, subvertising protests corporate greenwashing of fake environmental practices. Think of this as a form of artistic disobedience that redirects attention away from the hypnotic sleep-eat-work-consume state of modern life and leads us back to the three circles of life support: habitat, people, and story. It's vital work.

IT'S YOUR CULTURE TOO...

There's immense power and energy in the realization that no one really owns culture. In fact, everyone is a participant and a creator. To be sure, some voices are more influential than others, and it's great to have a megaphone if you can get one. And it's also the case that cultural gatekeepers will do whatever they can to sustain the status quo. But you're a creator with a voice as well. Every story you tell, every decision you make, every relationship you nurture or abandon; these all contribute to the reinforcement or transformation of culture. Stop assuming that you're powerless and get to work.

GOOD TROUBLE

The problem is that incrementalism is too small an ask. Not just too small to drive transformation; not just too small to stop the tidal wave of revolutionary change rolling in from the opposite direction; but also too small to break the conspiracy of silence. Only a demand for system change, directly confronting the power driving us to planetary destruction, has the potential to match the scale of the problem and to inspire and mobilize the millions of people required to generate effective action.

George Monbiot
The Guardian

As aspiring martial artists venturing into the world of conflict, it's natural to wonder about the reach of our methods. How audacious should we be? Should we aspire to do a little or a lot? Should we tinker around the edges of the issue in question or completely rework the system at its core? Should we take an incremental approach or go all in on rebellion and revolution?

Conventional wisdom suggests that incrementalism might be a good first choice. Drastic change is destabilizing to the human psyche and can trigger counterproductive fear responses, dysfunctional behavior, and chaos. The human animal needs some sense of social stability to feel safe, and small changes are simply easier for people to absorb, metabolize, and manage. Take baby steps—a little here, a little there, and after a few years or decades, systems will change for the better. This is the conservative approach.

All of which makes some kind of sense, but the obvious questions come quickly: What if incrementalism doesn't work? What if conditions are so dire that drastic change is needed to ensure our survival? What if a radical response is actually the rational response to catastrophic climate change and habitat destruction? And what if the conventional political process is stagnant, corrupt, and dysfunctional? In these conditions, baby steps may well be a distraction and a waste of precious time.

THE CASE AGAINST INCREMENTALISM

An increasing number of scientists and activists now argue that large-scale systemic change is the only viable path to a functional future. According to the Intergovernmental Panel on Climate Change, "Mitigation and development goals cannot be met through incremental change." This implies big, highly disruptive changes to the major systems that drive the modern world: energy, transportation, agriculture, and, above all, the economy. In other words, a ground-up revision to industry, capitalism, and even civilization itself.

The problem with incrementalism is twofold. Not only is it excruciatingly slow, it also lulls many of us into a false sense of security and comfort. It's easy to convince ourselves that minor lifestyle and political tweaks will eventually add up to something significant, so we lapse back into security and familiarity, content with the illusion that at least we're doing something. And, in the process, nothing really changes. We're just rearranging the deck chairs on the planetary lifeboat.

This, of course, is the metaphor for our times. If you're in a lifeboat and someone is chopping a hole in the hull, incrementalism is foolhardy. The water is gushing in and the craft is going down. Small tweaks to the process are only going to prolong the agony. To have a functional future, radical change is essential; really big things have to change, and fast. As climate activist Bill McKibben put it, "Winning slowly means losing."

And to reframe our perspective, many of us are coming to realize that the thing that's truly dangerous is the status quo itself—our modern, capitalistic, industrialized, hole-chopping, future-hostile system. From this perspective, overthrowing and transforming such a system and transforming it into something sustainable and functional is best seen, not as a radical act but a conservative, humanitarian, and pro-future position. In this sense, there's nothing extreme about revolutionary action. You're simply working for a functional, livable world.

THE PERILS OF OBEDIENCE

A related challenge is the fact that our existing social and cultural systems are massively gummed up with obedience and blind compliance. Most of us have been raised to believe that obedience is a mark of good character and an important element in social function, but it's also true that obedience has a nasty, highly destructive shadow side. In fact, obedience can pave the way for atrocity—to other human beings and even to the planet as a whole.

The most obvious example comes from the legendary

work of social psychologist Stanley Milgram, described in his landmark book *Obedience to Authority*. As Milgram discovered, human beings can be incredibly compliant in the face of authority and will even override their own moral sensibilities and judgment. When a white-coated authority figure demands that we comply with a task that will hurt other people, we're likely to do as we're told.

This sets the stage for all manner of bad behavior. As Milgram put it:

> The essence of obedience consists in the fact that a person comes to view himself as the instrument for carrying out another person's wishes. He therefore no longer regards himself as responsible for his actions.

In other words, the obedient person is no longer an activist, but a mere agent for someone else's plans and vision.

Milgram's work focused primarily on obedience in interpersonal relationships, but we can be certain that it also has destructive consequences in the domain of habitat destruction and ecocidal behavior. Industrial agriculture, industrial fishing, deforestation, mining, and fossil fuel development all require large organizations, staffed with compliant workers and managers who dutifully carry out their orders. It's impossible to measure, but we can be certain that a large proportion of future-hostile corporate behavior is only possible because of obedient workers and compliant consumers. As the street artist Banksy put it, "The greatest crimes in the world are not committed by people breaking the rules but by people following the rules."

THE ART OF DISOBEDIENCE

So what's to be done? Nearly every informed activist now agrees that widespread, systemic transformation is the only viable path to a functional future. Conventional protests and appeals to power don't seem to be working, so it's time to create some trouble—especially what civil rights activist John Lewis called "good trouble." To put it another way, it's time to create smart, intentional, and meaningful trouble. Trouble with a purpose and a vision. Trouble with a future.

This is a call for nonviolent civil disobedience, the intentional disruption of business, government, and culture-as-usual. It means interrupting conventional conversations and keeping people focused on the most urgent priorities of our day. The value of this practice is that it disturbs the flow of power in society and public perceptions about what may or may not be ethically acceptable. As Martin Luther King, Jr., put it, the objective is to "dramatize the conflict so that it can no longer be ignored."

Captain Paul Watson of the Sea Shepherd Conservation Society has blockaded and harassed whalers and factory fisheries on the open seas for years, in a practice he calls "aggressive nonviolence." For Watson, the goal is to "obstruct, intervene, interfere, harass…." It means accepting risk, getting in the face of adversaries, and calling out their crimes—but never engaging in violence to humans or non-human animals.

It's hard to say how effective these tactics have been, but the biggest benefit may actually be indirect. Civil disobedience may not substantially change the immediate behavior of your adversary, but it will communicate to others the seriousness of your resolve and your willingness to take risks for the sake of the future. In other words, the real targets of your action may well be people on the perimeter of the action.

This is why our stance, spirit, and character are so important. Bystanders will witness your tree-sit, your road blockade, or your lockdown at a bank or government office. They'll be curious about your position on the issue in question, but even more important, they'll be alert for the tone and tenor of your message, especially your courage or lack thereof. In this sense, *the details of your action may be less important than the dignity and resolve that you bring to the doing.* This is why civil disobedience is about much more than tactics. In essence, it's a spiritual practice. You're a role model and a representative, not just for your own movement, but for others who share similar values.

SMART TROUBLE

Civil disobedience is vital for our planetary health and the creation of a functional future, but it would be foolish to simply resist everything in our way. We're passionate about our cause, and we get frustrated with conditions, so we start advocating for change. But nothing seems to happen, and our frustration mounts by the day. Little by little, we drift ever closer to militancy and extremism. Actions that would have seemed unthinkable just a short time ago now seem like the only viable option. In our desperation, we can only see one path forward: tear down the entire system.

But it doesn't take much foresight or historical awareness to see how totalistic "solutions" might unfold. Even in the unlikely event that the revolution goes smoothly, the power vacuum at the other end is bound to be unstable, and unsustainable. This is why revolutions are so often followed by authoritarian, autocratic regimes; when all is chaos, someone's going to step into the void and take control.

So take a breath. A generalized disobedience to all authority might well be satisfying, but it's not going to get us very far. Instead, we've got to focus our disobedience with precision. Do you really want to burn down the entire system? What exactly are you disobeying and why? What's the ultimate target of your good trouble? Can you imagine the consequences of success? What comes after the revolution? Is there a plan for the aftermath?

The devil, as always, is in the details—or, more accurately, the lack of details. The revolutionary spirit is noble and necessary, but there has to be some thought of tomorrow. It's not enough to simply revolt. In fact, it's easy to imagine the kind of brutal ecological and social consequences that might come about in the wake of a totalistic revolution. When people are desperate, the last thing they'll be thinking about is preserving habitat or taking care of the human world. There has to be a plan for what comes next.

ENDS AND MEANS

So where to begin? You've got an issue and an objective, and you're ready for some kind of action, but what exactly are you going to do? Are you going to organize protests, hang banners, block financial institutions, or lock yourself down to construction equipment? And what kind of spirit are you going to bring to the action itself?

All of these questions bring us to the age-old issue of ends and means. You've got a goal in mind, an objective, but the question remains: are your means—your actions—consistent with that end? Some people say that, in exceptional circumstances, the end goal is so important and urgent that it justifies using drastic, exceptionally destructive means to get there. *Just get the job done,* they tell us, *no matter what it takes.* Others will object to this line of thinking and point to the danger that comes from such a view; if you believe that your chosen end justifies any means to get there, you step onto a slippery slope that leads to all kinds of toxic and destructive consequences. In the end, you may well defeat yourself.

This is why moral philosophers often teach that our means—our actions—should be congruent and consistent with our goals. As Mahatma Gandhi put it, ends and means are inseparable. "Realization of the goal is in exact proportion to that of the means…As the means, so the end." In other words, the quality of the journey inevitably shapes the destination. As Aldous Huxley wrote: "Good ends, as I have frequently to point out, can be achieved only by the employment of appropriate means. The end cannot justify the means, for the simple and obvious reason that the means employed determine the nature of the ends produced."

In other words, our actions must be crafted, intentionally and consciously, with the end in mind. It's bad practice to simply lash out and tear down with abandon. Passion and commitment are powerful, essential forces, but they can also warp our judgment. So slow down and consider the totality of your goals and actions. Could my actions stand alone as representative of what I'm trying to create? Look at your writing, your speech, your lockdown, your protest. Are these actions consistent with the end result you'd like to see? Are they beautiful or inspiring? If so, carry on.

REMEMBER THIS...

The prospect of making good trouble is both exhilarating and intimidating. You'll probably be excited and stressed in anticipation, but don't forget the fact that you're doing essential and honorable work. You aren't just sticking a spoke in the wheels of industry and corporate control; you're actually creating the future. You aren't just tearing down; you're also building up. So remember this: *a world of inconvenient truths calls for inconvenient people*, people who understand our predicament and are willing to disrupt convention. Be audacious in your thinking and your imagining. This is no time for thinking small. Be an inconvenient animal.

BE LIKE WATER

One can function freely and totally if he is "beyond system." The man who is really serious, with the urge to find out what truth is, has no style at all. He lives only in what is.

Bruce Lee

Imagine an adversary, an opponent, an enemy. Now imagine this person or organization does something outrageous and abusive, something that traumatizes you and violates everything you hold dear. It's natural to feel angry, furious, and you'll be quick to focus on his bad behavior and the many reasons he must be defeated.

In fact, your assessment may well be right on the mark. Your adversary might truly be as nasty, corrupt, and toxic as you say. But there's also danger in this perspective. Your emotion—no matter how accurate or justified—can cloud your judgment, compromise your performance, and lead you into catastrophic error.

The problem with adversaries is that they don't just threaten our bodies, our possessions, and our values, they also capture our minds and spirits. Their behavior strikes us as outrageous, and completely outside the bounds of human decency. They have no right to behave the way they do, no justification for their actions or their attitude. They must be crazy or evil or both. We become indignant and self-righteous, and, in the process, our emotion begins to tyrannize our consciousness, our imagination, and even our bodies. Our adversaries don't just threaten our welfare; they also send us into vicious cycles of fear, projection, rumination, obsession, and demonizing. Before long, our performance collapses, and we become ineffective, or worse.

To be sure, some adversaries are worthy of all the animosity we can muster, but you've got to be careful. Disgust and hatred may be well-deserved, but it doesn't help your performance. This is why teachers in traditional martial arts sometimes reframe conflict and remind their students that "the enemy is never wrong."

This concept may sound alien, if not completely preposterous. Of course your adversary is a monster. Of course he's operating outside the bounds of decent human behavior. Of course he's devious and maybe even evil. Let's accept all that for the moment. But suppose that, instead of getting obsessed with your adversary's outrageousness, you relax and concentrate on the basic reality of his or her behavior. Focus on solutions. What it's going to take to set things right? How you feel is important, but intelligent action is the real issue.

THE STYLE OF NO STYLE

The value in this kind of detachment is that it allows us to see our opponents clearly, without prejudice, expectation, or prediction. Our adversaries are fundamentally unpredictable agents who are capable of anything, so the less we assume about them the better. This is particularly true in the world of traditional martial arts, where teachers remind us to let go of our emotion and expectations about the way things should be. Get your mind out of the way and let your highly-trained highly trained body do the work.

As a human animal, your adversary is capable of almost anything. That's why the ideal response is fluidity in motion—pure creativity, pure adaptability, and pure improv. Bruce Lee himself argued for maximum flexibility in combat, and even started his own art form: *Jeet Kune Do*, the "style of no style."

"Empty your mind," he taught. "Be formless, shapeless, like water. If you put water into a cup, it becomes the cup. You put water into a bottle and it becomes the bottle. You put it in a teapot, it becomes the teapot. Now water can flow, or it can crash. Be water, my friend."

THE WORLD IS NEVER WRONG

This all makes good sense in the world of hand-to-hand combat, but is even more powerful when we apply it to the totality of our human experience. What if we practiced this kind of emotional detachment on a larger scale? Just imagine a life in which

People are never wrong.

Culture is never wrong.

Events are never wrong.

Laws and policies are never wrong.

Your personal experience and emotions are never wrong.

The people in your life are never wrong.

Your anxiety, stress, and depression are never wrong.

Your injuries and illnesses are never wrong.

Imagine how you'd feel if you looked at the world this way. The rightness or wrongness of your situation would be irrelevant and, in turn, powerless to distract you. You'd be free to see clearly and act effectively, without friction, stress, resistance, or anxiety. Paradoxically perhaps, giving up your mental and emotional resistance will actually make you a better fighter.

To be sure, this perspective can never be easy, pure, or absolute, nor would we want it to be. We are emotional animals after all, and we're sensitive to injustices of all kinds. We want life to be fair and we're quick to react, sometimes powerfully and passionately, to negative events, especially those we consider unjust. Our bodies respond instinctively, driven by ancient, legacy programming beyond the reach of conscious control. It would be nonhuman to stand completely apart from life and view it all with cold objectivity.

Nevertheless, a little detachment can go a long way. Can you pause and step back for a moment? Can you see your predicament without judgment or expectation? Can you adopt the perspective of a scientist or a journalist and see the thing in question just as it is? Take a breath, relax, and imagine no judgment.

You can practice this orientation in meditation. Just sit quietly for a few minutes and pay attention. Thoughts, images, and emotions will come, and some will be unwelcome, but don't resist. Don't try to change anything. Your experience is never wrong, your animal body is never wrong, your mind is never wrong. Simply return your attention to your breath and feel what you're feeling. As the Buddhist teacher Jack Kornfield put it, "Let go of the battle. Breathe quietly and let it be. Let your body relax and your heart soften. Open to whatever you experience without fighting." Accept what is happening, and before long your mind and body will relax. When this happens, you'll be ready to re-engage with clarity and creativity.

WHAT THIS IS NOT

This sense of non-attachment is a powerful and vital orientation, but caution is also in order. That is, this is not an argument for apathy, passivity, or an uncritical acceptance of everything in the world. Some things on this planet are wickedly, morally wrong and must be opposed with all the power we can muster. Fighting remains essential, honorable, and sapient. We must never forget the atrocities that have been committed and that continue to be perpetrated on people, animals, and the planet. The historical memory of such events is truly sacred.

Nevertheless, this "never wrong" approach remains a highly functional perspective. The sooner we accept the reality of negative events, ideas, people, and experiences, the sooner we can get to work devising effective strategies and tactics. This radical realism leaves preference and expectation behind. Let go of the angst; deal with reality and your adversary without illusion. Observe, relax, and move.

Outrage has its place, but sometimes the best course is to play the situation as it stands. Life is capable of anything. People are capable of anything. Humans are highly complex animals, struggling to live in an alien, highly stressful environment. We're driven by ancient impulses that sometimes bubble to the surface, leading us to behave in some strange and incomprehensible ways. Everyone is irrational.

We'd all like to have things a certain way, but our preferences are not the issue. Our job is to create and re-create adaptations on the fly. When we get too wrapped up in the wrongness of people, organizations, or events, we become rigid and lose our sapience. We lose our ability to move and, in turn, become even more vulnerable. If we can let go of our indignation, we can start fresh and return to the encounter with a clear vision. As the spiritual teacher Jiddu Krishnamurti put it, "Do you want to know what my secret is? I don't mind what happens."

REMEMBER THIS...

As a stress-relieving practice, this reframe is almost magical. As soon as we say, "Reality is never wrong," our minds turn around, and a lot of our angst simply disappears, at least for a while. The conflict and the danger may persist, but the anger and indignation lose their ability to tyrannize us. In turn, this frees us up to bring more of our resources to bear on doing what needs to be done. So whatever you do, keep your eye on the what is.

DEEP AND WIDE

A specialist's mind is a slave to his specialization.

Mokokoma Mokhonoana

The activist engages the world with great ambition and sense of purpose, but before long, things are likely to get complex, murky, and ambiguous. Battle lines will shift, adversaries will change their tactics, and even our priorities will change. If we're going to succeed, we've got to stay focused on our core issue, before complexity and noise drive us into a state of confusion, if not outright distraction.

The challenge is particularly acute in today's world, where our attention has been broken into a thousand fragments. To say that we're distracted doesn't even begin to describe it. Everyone's drinking from the digital fire hose now, suffering from acute levels of cognitive overload. Not only does this cause us massive levels of stress, it also sabotages our ability to learn and act effectively.

So it is for the young activist. There are so many overlapping crises now, so many wicked, interdependent issues that demand our attention. There's a glut of urgent, compelling battles to be fought, and each one feels like a nightmare of complexity. We study our favorite issues and prepare for our most important engagements, but we're distracted by other related problems that feel equally important. We want to fight those battles too—but who has the bandwidth and energy for all that?

As you've surely heard by now, the human mind has a very limited capacity for multitasking. When we attempt to do too much, the mind tries to keep up by rapidly switching from one task to another. In the beginning, we can keep up, but before long, the effort collapses into confusion and, ultimately, exhaustion. That's why coaches, teachers, and tribal elders often caution us to focus on one thing at a time. The Latin poet writer Publilius Syrus once quipped, "To do two things at once is to do neither." Likewise, an African parable tells us, "A good hunter does not chase two rabbits." To fight a dozen battles is to lose them all.

THE GAMBLE

Living on the edge of overwhelm, we try to fight back by narrowing our focus to issues and battles that we might be able to control. And on the face of it, specialization appears to be a good practice. If we can tighten our focus on one issue at a time, we can bring more of our attention to the battle in question. Choose a favorite issue—climate, biodiversity, oceans, forests, reproductive rights, gun safety, education, or human health—and drill down as far as you can. Know the issue intimately and you'll have a chance for success.

But there are dangers here as well. In a radically interconnected, nonlinear world, specialization is always risky because there really are no isolated, stand-alone issues, agents, or events. Everything is overlapping, moving, and interdependent, so it's hard to know where to focus. Shouldn't we also be keeping our eyes on the wider panorama of attention and action?

This tension between specializing and generalizing isn't

just relevant to activism; it's universal in the human experience. It's the dilemma faced by every gambler, every gold prospector, every fisherman, every online dater, and every person who's encountering an ambiguous predicament. Shall I put my energy, time, and bets down on a single spot, or should I spread myself out over the terrain and hope that I strike it rich?

The dilemma is obvious. If you dig a deep hole in just the right place, you might hit the jackpot. But if you dig in the wrong spot, you'll waste years of your life and come up empty-handed. If you specialize too narrowly, you might be digging a very deep hole in the wrong place, but if you take on every issue, you'll spread yourself too thin, and you won't be effective at any of it. In this case, your activism will be a mile wide and an inch deep. Plus, no one individual has the time or resources to fight on every front. You might become a jack-of-all-trades, but sometimes you really need to be a master of one.

Everyone seems to have their own style and preferences. Some of us like to choose a single issue and dig deep; others like to travel widely and take a deeper dive every now and then. But sadly, we receive almost no guidance on how to navigate this challenge. Schools teach isolated subjects, and rarely, if ever, are students encouraged to develop an overarching meta strategy for dealing with the broad terrain of human knowledge and action. Typically, school is mostly a flood of information, some of it broad, some of it deep, and we're just expected to know it all.

Consequently, students generally have no idea which direction to go. Will I be rewarded for specializing, or should I wander far afield in my search? Students are whipsawed from one orientation to the other, never sure how deep to dig or how far to wander. Not surprisingly, many of us end up zigging and zagging through life, sometimes specializing, sometimes generalizing, but mostly going on impulse and hope. All of which gets us nowhere, or worse.

MEET THE T

The good news is that there is a strategy that puts our efforts together in a sensible form, one that works across a variety of domains, including activism and martial artistry. Think of the letter "T." The horizontal bar implies surveying the landscape, maybe digging a series of shallow holes here and there, but mostly just wandering and taking things in. The vertical axis suggests choosing a specialization, digging a hole in that one spot, and going as deep as possible.

This T model goes a long way toward giving our activism a functional shape and orientation. The idea is that by balancing wide-ranging exploration with a single, focused discipline, we put ourselves in a position for success. As biologist Thomas Henry Huxley famously put it, "Try to learn everything about something and something about everything."

The T model is often used in professional training, where doctors and attorneys face similar challenges of navigating vast domains of knowledge. But it also makes sense in the world of activism, and in principle, it's simple: The vertical bar represents your most important issue, your alpha battle. The horizontal bar refers to all the other activism that's going on in the world. In practice, each effort complements the other to form a functional whole. The vertical effort gives you a disciplined look at how one process works, while the horizontal effort keeps you aware of how everything else behaves.

Notice that our horizontal and vertical efforts each have a very different feel. The vertical effort feels focused, deliberate, and intentional. You're in hot pursuit of specific, relevant knowledge that will serve your objective. There's no time for distraction, play, or levity. You know what you want, and you're going after it. This is disciplined work.

In contrast, the horizontal effort feels more casual and opportunistic. You're wandering the landscape, sampling what's out there, observing the diversity of methods and philosophies you encounter along the way. In this state, you don't mind getting distracted, as you never know what kind of juicy discoveries you might make. Daydreams and brainstorms are welcome. If the vertical is hard-focused, the horizontal is soft-focused. You're curious, filled with wonder about what lies just over the horizon.

VERTICAL AND HORIZONTAL ACTIVISM

All of which can go a long way towards giving our activism a functional form. When we work with the T, our efforts become rhythmic, coherent, and sustainable. Alternating between depth and breadth keeps us focused, curious, and engaged. Ultimately, we'll be more relaxed and effective; our choices will become more intentional and productive.

The first step is to decide on your alpha issue and start digging. Focus intensely on your passion project. Suppose your alpha issue is new fossil fuel development. You've decided that this is a crucial issue, one that deserves your attention and focus, so you study the facts, the history, the players, the policies, and the leverage points. Along the way, you're bound to encounter intimidating levels of complexity, but stay disciplined. When chaos strikes, stay with the effort and don't get distracted. Protect your attentional resources and defend your inquiry. When new and distracting possibilities come into view, ask yourself, *"Is this new inquiry aligned with my vision?"* Be selective and triage your efforts.

But don't stop there. The next step is to take a break and widen your search. Get out of your own domain for a while and study other activists' efforts, even those you disagree with. How do other people and organizations succeed in changing minds, laws, or policies? What worked for others and what didn't? Don't get distracted by your personal preferences and beliefs. You may find other people's values and positions revolting, and you may well take issue with their methods, but you can still learn from their experience. How did your adversary manage to score a victory? Or, why was he or she defeated?

Suppose your alpha issue is gun control and gun safety. How do gun rights advocates manage to succeed? Maybe your issue is women's reproductive rights—how do anti-choice forces manage to win their battles? Maybe your issue is habitat and species preservation—how do pro-development organizations manage to win so many victories over the earth and the future? This effort will enlarge your thinking and give you a broader understanding of what's possible.

REMEMBER THIS...

Naturally, everyone has their own preferences and styles, all, depending on history, culture, and personality. Some of us are born to dig deep on the vertical axis; others are more suited to wandering the horizontal. All of which requires some introspection and observation. Are you a driller or a wanderer? Are you looking for the certainty and control that comes with mastery of a particular domain, or are you more interested in the vast panorama of knowledge that lies just over the horizon?

This understanding is crucial, but even more important is the ability and the willingness to round out your practice by alternating between the horizontal and the vertical. If you feel most comfortable in one direction, try the other. In fact, a good general practice is to alternate intentionally and rhythmically between drilling and wandering. Spend a day or a season trying to know everything about something, then spend another trying to know something about everything.

Likewise, give some thought to your teams and alliances. The T model suggests that it's folly to surround yourself exclusively with like-minded people. If you're a verticalist by nature, having more vertical people on your team might well limit your vision and put you at risk for an unexpected blind side attack. If you're a horizontalist, having more wanderers in the mix won't give you an understanding of how any one thing really works. Instead, look for a diversity of perspectives to make your effort complete, whole, and powerful.

LISTEN UP

If you wanna speak like the gods, your ear must be open as the sky.

Writer Curtis Tyrone Jones

The activist is passionate about engaging the world and shaping the future, but to be effective, you've got to know your adversaries, the history and context of your battles, and the terrains of engagement. The more you understand, the more effective your actions are likely to be. Nothing is so dangerous as acting without comprehension. At best, you'll waste your time and energy; at worst, you'll inflame the system and make your battles a thousand times more dangerous.

Our ancestors understood this perfectly. Hunting and gathering in a wild setting is no easy task. To be successful, hunters had to pay attention to every sensation that might reveal something important about the ways of plants, animals, water, and weather. Modern paleo enthusiasts like to talk about the rigors of long-distance running and the pursuit of prey, but the essential skills were tracking, attention, and sensitivity. It's no wonder that, in traditional societies, children are taught to listen, to be quiet, and to be attentive to habitat. Tribal elders sometimes tell young people to *WAIT* before speaking, which stands for "Why Am I Talking?"

But in the modern world, it's precisely the opposite.

Sensitivity and listening have fallen out of favor and have been replaced by a cult of personal expression. We're encouraged to seek publicity and, above all, to be heard—even if our messages are harmful distortions or outright falsehoods. Talking is all the rage, and now that almost everyone has an Internet platform, modern life has come to resemble one vast cocktail party, with everyone talking at the top of their voices, stopping only to refill their drinks.

Even worse, our cinematic role models show little in the way of sensitivity. Action-adventure heroes wield muscle, weapons, and clever talk but rarely seem be attentive to much of anything. The protagonist leaps into action, takes charge, and dominates the situation, but how does he even know the nature of his engagement? Without sensation and receptivity, his body is little more than a muscular device for inflicting violence. Perhaps it's no wonder that there are so few listeners among us.

WHOLE BODY LISTENING

It would be a mistake to assume that listening is something done exclusively with the ears. In natural, premodern settings, the human animal feels the world with the entire body, operating in relationship with natural and social habitats. The body-brain system has often been likened to a machine or a computer, but more accurately, it's an incredibly sensitive learning instrument that can detect the most subtle variations in habitat and people around us. In other words, our intelligence isn't concentrated in our heads; it's spread out across the entire body, habitat, and society.

In natural settings, our senses operate holistically, each reinforcing the others to build a complete understanding of setting and circumstance. In contrast, modern humans spend immense amounts of time working a single visual channel in front of various devices, sometimes supplemented by audio. This amounts to a radical distortion of our normal sensorium; it's no wonder that so many of us suffer from anxiety and a fragmented sense of being. For the vast majority of our time on this planet, our senses have worked together, in tandem. Breaking them apart into single channels is profoundly dis-integrating and even dangerous.

It's true that we listen with our ears, but it's also true that we listen with our eyes. In particular, we observe the posture and facial expressions of people around us, relayed through mirror neurons in the brain. Not only do we see the movements of their others' bodies, we also sense the intent behind their actions. This information is transmitted deep into our bodies, where it's processed in our gut, specifically the enteric nervous system, sometimes described as "the body's second brain". This process allows us to, in effect, run a simulation of what other people are feeling and experiencing. Taken as a whole, this so-called resonance circuit forms a vital part of whole-body social sensitivity.

We listen with our skin, our taste receptors, and our sense of smell, and we even listen with our muscles. Few of us are aware of how powerful this process is. The musculoskeletal system is the largest sensory organ in the body and it's constantly giving us information, not just on the position and momentum of our own bodies, but on the shapes and characteristics of the things that we interact with. In our hyper-cognitive age, muscular learning is often ignored, but it's essential to awareness and effectiveness.

OBSTACLES

Unfortunately, the modern world presents myriad barriers that interfere with our efforts to sense, listen, and feel. We'd like to be receptive to the world, but sometimes it feels like we're being blocked at every turn.

Insulation is an obvious problem. We seek comfort behind walls, steel, and glass, but there's always a trade-off. The more protection we wrap around ourselves, the less we feel. Likewise, the near-universal plasticization of the modern world gives us a monotonous tactile experience; we touch smooth, uniform, and lifeless surfaces, without contrast and texture. In the process, nothing much registers in our brains.

Noise is another obvious offender, and it comes in a thousand forms. Leaf blowers and mowers dominate our neighborhoods, but cognitive overload also shuts down our receptivity. Busyness and stress derail our attention and our physical and social sensitivity. Ten thousand details force us into radical triage; if a sensory experience isn't immediately relevant to the demands of the moment, we simply reject it and move on.

These environmental obstacles to receptivity are substantial, but even more challenging are the psycho-philosophical orientations that keep us from taking in our surroundings. Listening is a physical act, but it also stems from our attitude, stance, posture, and relationship with the world at large.

Imagine that you've fallen in love with your understanding of the world, and you're absolutely confident in your knowledge and beliefs. You've lived a few decades, seen a few things, and you're certain that what you know is real, true, and reliable. And because your knowledge is complete in your eyes, you come to believe there's not much point in listening to anything or anyone else. Why even bother being receptive when there's nothing left to learn?

So too for our species as a whole, especially our assumption of superiority over the natural world. When we declare ourselves the alpha animal on the planet, why would we bother listening to our "subordinates" in the natural world? Shouldn't they be listening to us?

But this assumption of superiority isn't just ecologically foolish, it's also incredibly dangerous and self-defeating. To be effective, our sensitivity must come from a place of humility. If you want to experience the world, you've got to abandon the assumption that you already know it. In other words, the best course is to work from an assumption of ignorance; the less you "know," the more you'll be able to feel.

TURN IT AROUND

The sad reality is that most of what we call "listening" in the modern world is incredibly narrow. We're sometimes attentive to facts, ideas, and stories, but mostly we listen for information that confirms our preexisting worldviews. In psychological circles, this is known as "confirmation bias."

It's a very comforting and popular process. Like strange, new world hunter-gatherers, we scan the world for anything that will buttress and support what we already believe to be true. It's mostly unconscious, and it's probably even a human universal, but it's extremely corrosive to learning and progress. Over the years, this selective attention moves us ever closer to dogma and artificial certainty. We claim to know the world, but all we've collected is a mountain of confirmation. In the process, we become increasingly immobile and, ultimately, dangerous.

To be successful and effective, we need to reverse this tendency and replace it with what we might call a "contradiction bias." Like the scientists, the activist must be on the lookout, not for confirmation, but for evidence that falsifies his assumptions and worldviews. In other words, he actively listens for anything that might prove him wrong.

This is not an easy or popular path, but it's essential to effectiveness and integrity. As a working philosophy, confirmation doesn't get us very far, but contradiction forces us into productive revisions of our beliefs. The process might well be painful and upsetting, but that's beside the point. Listen for evidence that disproves your preexisting views, and you might actually get somewhere. Proving yourself wrong may not be pleasant, but it's far, far better than wandering into battle with a foolish sense of certainty.

REMEMBER THIS...

Ultimately, the challenge is to remain open and permeable to experience. Relinquish what you know, be skeptical of your beliefs, honor your ignorance, and let the understanding come to you. Feel the world as it is, then act.

RIPPLE EFFECTS

The least movement is of importance to all nature.
The entire ocean is affected by a pebble.

Blaise Pascal

French mathematician, philosopher, and physicist

1623–1662

As activists living and working in a vast and complex world, all of us desire certainty and predictability. We want our actions to produce tangible results that we can see, feel, or maybe even touch. But oddly, it rarely seems to work out that way, and over time, we begin to suspect that the world is not nearly so regular, orderly, and mechanical as we would like. One thing influences another, but often in mysterious and unpredictable ways. The ultimate effects of our actions might be modest, they might dissipate into nothing, or they might trigger some major event that's far out of proportion to the original act. It's difficult, maybe even impossible, to know what causes what.

This, of course, is known as the *butterfly effect*. Taken from the world of atmospheric science and complexity theory, scientists have discovered that small initial causes can have big downstream consequences. As we've heard in various forms, "the flap of a butterfly's wings in one region can set off a hurricane on the other side of the planet." It's an intriguing idea with big implications for our activism, our martial artistry, and the ways that we touch the world.

Suppose you're a first-time activist, headed out into the streets to protest. You make a clever sign and put it up for all to see. You chant and yell and maybe even get arrested. It's exciting, and it feels meaningful, but you wake up the next day to find that the world hasn't changed in any perceptible way. Even worse, your community and the media seems to have ignored your efforts entirely. You want to see an effect, but you're not seeing much of anything. Not surprisingly, you feel discouraged, and maybe you're even tempted to give up on the whole thing.

But maybe we aren't looking at this the right way. After all, activists of all stripes are working with immensely complex, interconnected systems—large organizations, societies, culture, and the public imagination. These systems are not linear machines that behave in predictable ways or that can be adjusted with the turn of a screw. No, these systems are hypercomplex and radically interdependent, which means they have more in common with things like atmospheres, ecosystems, and the human nervous system. In these domains, things work much differently than we might expect. In particular, we see that small, almost insignificant changes in initial conditions can cascade through the system to produce wildly disproportionate results.

In other words, activism is not physics—or, to be more precise, it's not Newtonian physics. The world is not a clock or a mechanism that behaves with consistent regularity; it's more like a living organism. Conditions are wickedly complex, and it's rarely possible to sort out strict chains of cause and effect. You'll never be able to say with certainty that a protest, letter-writing campaign, or act of civil disobedience produced a particular, well-defined result. Activism just doesn't work that way. It's not as if an expert can tell you, "Do this action and you'll get this outcome." At best, all we can really do is think in terms of probabilities, which is to say, every action is a gamble.

IMPLICATIONS

Butterfly effects make for some intriguing science, but this is about far more than the curious behavior of atmospheres and other hypercomplex systems. In fact, there are vital life lessons here that will go a long way toward shaping our activism, our martial artistry, and even the trajectory of our lives as a whole. Consider these implications:

You're never going to know as much as you'd like. Radical complexity tells us that we will always be largely ignorant about the world around us. When working with massively interdependent systems, there are simply too many moving parts and relationships to track. You can do all the homework you want and harness as much computing power as you can afford, but your knowledge is likely to remain fragmentary and incomplete at best.

There's simply no way to know precisely how your actions will affect the world. A massively researched, highly organized, well-funded effort might fall flat, but a small gesture might ripple through a social system and transform another person's life a thousand miles away. In a hyperdynamic world, things can change in a heartbeat, and predictions are likely to be unreliable.

Expertise is minimally useful. Sophisticated knowledge, no matter how well developed, can never go as far as we might like. Specialists and professionals can make some good guesses, but these are mostly probabilities. Even the most well-informed mind can only grok a fraction of the whole, and many expert predictions turn out to be just plain wrong.

Control is mostly an illusion. Even if we do manage to find our way into conventional social power, we still don't have nearly as much control over events as we'd like. You might manage some minor influence over local situations, but hypercomplex systems are simply too big for any one person or organization to understand, much less control.

Judgment calls are everywhere. Since our knowledge, expertise, and control are inherently limited by complexity, we have no choice but to rely on personal judgment, over and over, throughout the course of our lives. Even for the smartest and most diligent of activists, life will always be a series of judgment calls. Get used to it.

You're touching the entire world. Even the smallest action can ripple all the way across the planet and forward in time to future generations. Everything we say or do is potentially significant and maybe even powerful. In essence, there are no meaningless actions. Everything we do matters.

HUMILITY AND POWER

All of us desire knowledge, certainty, and predictability, but the butterfly world offers none of these things. We want to see quick and concrete results, but complexity suggests that the consequences of our actions may be distant and remote in space and time. Our actions may amount to nothing, or they might ripple around the planet and transform someone we will never meet. Or, the cascade might extend deep into the future, driving changes in the minds, bodies, or cultures of our descendants.

The lesson here is that you might well be more powerful than you realize. In our conventional perspective, many of us are quick to be intimidated by the sheer magnitude of the various systems and organizations that we're fighting against. You're just one person up against a vast corporation, a bureaucracy, a media empire, or entrenched culture. You might well feel insignificant and helpless.

But are you really? Isn't this simply an assumption, a belief based on nothing? How can you possibly know the ultimate consequences of your behavior? In a butterfly world, you never really know. In this way, your assumption of powerlessness is really a misunderstanding of how the world works. You might well be moving the needle on the world, and not know it. You might well be more powerful than you believe.

YOU NEVER KNOW...

Our understanding of the butterfly effect naturally leads us towards the traditional virtues of patience, modesty, and humility that are common in wisdom traditions. So relax into your ignorance and insecurity. Don't be frustrated with an apparent lack of results. You may not be able to control the world, but you *can* control the way you show up. You may not feel powerful, but you can always act with sincerity, resolve, and integrity. You may not understand the totality of your predicament or the ultimate consequences of your actions, but you can always pay attention.

So do the best you can. Touch the world with sincerity and let things unfold as they will. Make your best guess, act with integrity, and let your spirit ripple through the system. You may not be around to see the ultimate results, but rest assured, you *are* making a difference. The way you show up *is* the way you change the world.

THE RIGHT TOUCH

Your hand opens and closes, opens and closes. If
it were always a fist or always stretched open, you
would be paralyzed. Your deepest presence is in
every small contracting and expanding, the two
as beautifully balanced and coordinated as birds'
wings.

Rumi

The butterfly flaps its wings and sets off a cascade of
consequences that ripple across the world. The effects
might be modest, they might dissipate into nothing, or
they might trigger some major event that's far out of proportion to the original act. As we've seen, this effect has big
implications for our activism, our martial artistry, and the
ways that we touch the world. But what is that right touch?
What does it feel like, and why do we so rarely talk about it?
The quality of our touch will go a long way towards determining our success or failure as activists, but sadly, we almost never teach any of this. It's almost certain that you've
never taken a class called How to Touch the World. If we
do happen to learn this art, we do it by stumbling through
the world, suffering through awkward trial and error. It's
no wonder that we so often get it wrong, swinging back and
forth between passivity, aggression, and violence, between
under- and overreactions to circumstance.

Lacking education and training in this art, most of us are

quick to revert to the familiar. We touch the world, not by conscious intention and training, but by way of our history, personality, habits, or culture. For better or for worse, our parents, siblings, teachers, and coaches have given us ideas about ways how to interact. If your role models touched the world in a particular way, there's a good chance that you'll carry on the tradition, whether it's passive, assertive, or aggressive. And whatever the details, you can be certain that the quality of your touch will be contagious, cascading through whatever social system you happen to inhabit.

INVERSE U

So how should the martial artist touch a world that's in constant motion, filled with uncertainty, ambiguity, and judgment calls? Is there a general principle that we can work with? Perhaps there is. Almost everywhere we look, from habitats and ecosystems to human and animal physiology, we find an inverse U-shaped curve of benefit.

According to this model, a small amount of something may be beneficial, and a little more might be really powerful, but there's always a tipping point and a descent into the realm of diminishing returns. Drink a little water or eat a little food; that's good. Eat or drink a little more; even better. But beyond the sweet spot, you're going to get into trouble. This principle holds in all kinds of domains, and it's safe to assume that it would also hold true in the way we touch the world at large.

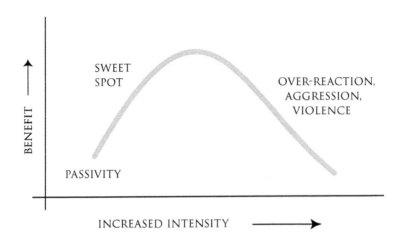

Consider an inverse U for touch. At the extreme left side of the graph lies passivity. You're engaged in some kind of conflict or drama, but you don't fight back at all—physically, verbally, or emotionally. You just go limp or simply avoid the entire confrontation in the hope of avoiding any risk. Quite obviously, there's danger here for both body and spirit. Allowing people to walk all over us is never a good practice, and in the long run, there's a lot to lose.

That said, this practice might well be appropriate for what we might call strategic passivity and non-resistance. When faced with overwhelming force in a street protest, for example, you might choose to make a point by going limp, allowing yourself to be arrested and carried away. Fighting back might be folly in such a circumstance, but you can still make a statement with your passive resistance. This may well be a good choice in acts of civil disobedience.

Going up the left side of the inverse U, we touch the world with more power, more strength and intensity. This is where we're likely to find the optimal level of action, force, and influence. We're neither passive nor aggressive, but assertive. You may be afraid or intimidated, but you're determined to take a stand, protect your interests, and draw boundaries. You're speaking clearly and maintaining a solid stance. This is your time to have a say, so seize it. *This is who I am, this is what I believe, this is what I'm asking, this is my position.* You may not be comfortable in this assertive stance, but it's something you can learn with experience.

Going over the top of the inverse U, we descend into the world of diminishing returns, overreaction, overcompensation, and, ultimately, violence. At this point, there's no thought of proportion or balance. The aim is to inflict maximum damage or simply destroy our adversary. This is a heavy touch, an act of aggression.

Sadly, this is what we see in so many action-adventure movies in which the protagonist extracts revenge in the most spectacular way possible. But even worse, it's an apt description of the way we treat the planet. There's no attempt to understand, no attempt to harmonize with life-supporting processes. Rather, we seek to dominate the natural world with dams, highways, fossil-fuel infrastructure, industrial agriculture, and industrial fishing. All of which lies at the far right of the inverse U—a heavy, brutal touch.

In any case, there's a powerful lesson here. The inverse U will never tell us exactly what to do in a conflict, but it can remind us that small adjustments might bring us back into the sweet spot of assertive touch. Experience will help, but simply asking the right questions will go a long way:

- What kind of response is appropriate here and now?

- How much adversarial energy should I bring to this encounter?

- Will I revert to habit, or can I create something intentional and proportional?

You may well get it wrong at first, and you'll probably under- and overcorrect on occasion, but with experience, you'll learn to narrow down the error and maybe even get it right. Bring the right spirit to the encounter and you'll have a chance.

HARD OR SOFT?

In the world of strategy, tactics, and traditional martial art, there's a lot of talk about the differences between *hard style* and *soft style*. What kind of force should we bring to a conflict? Is it better to hammer your adversary with focused strikes or blend with his movement and turn it to your advantage? Each style has its place, but it's important to recognize that there are advantages and dangers in *both* directions.

Hard style includes movements, speech, attitudes, and actions that, in the language of the traditional martial arts, "meet force with force." The power of this approach lies in its clarity and simplicity. The word "no"—in all its various manifestations—sends a clear, unambiguous message: "This is a boundary. You may not cross this boundary. If you cross this boundary, I am going to fight back. You will suffer unpleasant consequences." This kind of action may well be necessary for self-protection or for the defense of others, including our life-support systems. When used appropriately, it's a useful, practical, even healthy skill.

If you choose a hard style response, commitment is vital.

Whether verbal or physical, it's important to be loud and clear about where your boundaries lie. When you make the decision to act, don't waver; go all in. Speak with conviction and confidence, backed up by assertive body language and posture. If under physical assault, use a *kiai*, the famous shout used in traditional martial arts. Bring all your psycho-physical energy together into a single, integrated, and powerful act.

But, of course, hard style responses aren't always appropriate, especially when they're impulsive. When we become angry or fearful, we lose our sense of proportion, and in the extreme, our hard style responses can become ugly. When we fight fire with fire, things tend to escalate, and it's all wickedly contagious. In the process, you may well inspire your adversary to increase his resistance and retaliate. Even if you happen to win a particular encounter, you've inflamed the system and increased the chances that you'll have to suffer hard style actions coming back the other way.

As for *soft style*, a common prescription tells us to "use the enemy's strength against him." If you can amplify or exaggerate your opponents' movements, you can lead him out of balance and into a state of instability. From there it becomes easy—in theory at least—to turn his movements into a fall or to pin him to the ground.

The quintessential expressions of the soft-style approach come from the Taoist tradition, most notably from Lao-tzu in his great classic, the *Tao Te Ching*:

> The highest good is like water...Nothing in the world is softer and weaker than water. Yet there is nothing better for subduing all that is harder and stronger.

What you want to compress you must first truly
allow to expand. What you want to weaken you
must first allow to grow strong. What you want to
destroy you must first allow to truly flourish. From
whoever you want to take away, you must first truly
give. This is called being clear about the invisible.
The soft wins victory over the hard. The weak wins
victory over the strong.

In conversation or political discourse, you might think of
this soft-style approach as *hyperagreement*. Instead of opposing your adversaries' position with a counterargument,
encourage his extremity. Blend with his language; amplify
and exaggerate his ideas and reasoning. As Sun Tzu put it,
"Pretend inferiority and encourage his arrogance." Help
him take his opinions, movements, and actions to the point
of absurdity and reversal. At some point, he'll either realize
his folly or lapse into a state of frustration and confusion.

It's a seductive idea, and in some cases, it can be a practical, effective solution. It might even be useful when a
smaller and weaker David goes up against a vastly more
powerful Goliath. The beauty of this approach is that—if
executed with a high level of skill—it doesn't inflame or
provoke a counterreaction. When perfectly executed, your
opponents essentially throws himself.

But there are substantial caveats and real dangers here. If
you're too soft or awkward in your response, you may be
overwhelmed. If you misread your adversary's intentions
or fail to turn his movement to your advantage, all may be
lost. In fact, the soft style approach requires an exceptionally high level of training, skill, understanding, and attention.
If you want to use your adversary's movement against him,
you've got to know precisely where he's going and what he's

trying to accomplish.

This suggests that you've got to be a dedicated student of your adversary, his history, values, ideology, and circumstances. What moves my opponent? What are his objectives? What's his stance and position? What's the trajectory of his behavior? The more understanding you have, the better. Once you know your adversary, his intentions, and his inclinations and movement arcs, you're in a good position to help him go to extremes, and maybe even throw himself in the process. In an odd way, empathy and understanding might even be the key to victory.

Above all, this soft style calls for a spirit of non-attachment and psycho-spiritual flexibility. To execute a successful blend, you've got to abandon your personal likes and dislikes, at least for a while. Read your enemies, get inside their minds, relinquish your preferences and adopt their movements as your own. The more complete your blend, the easier it will be to nudge them in a new direction.

AMBIDEXTERITY

Naturally, people are quick to argue about the merits of hard and soft styles, and many will claim that one is superior to the other. But out in the real world, the martial artist must be versatile and capable of both. Our adversaries are in a constant state of flux, and it's hard to predict what they might do. If all you've got is one style, you're going to be limited, ineffective, and, ultimately, vulnerable.

In other words, it's best to be ambidextrous and enter each encounter with a sense of balance and equipoise—neither violent nor passive, but assertive. You've got a plan and an objective, but you're capable of changing your movements and your intent on the fly. If soft doesn't work, be ready for something more direct. If hard doesn't work, turn down the heat and see if a blend might be more effective.

REMEMBER THIS...

Ultimately, right touch comes from holding the right spirit, in your mind and body. What's your intent? How do you feel about the world at large? How do you feel about this particular engagement or action? Do you want to destroy the opposition, blend with their movements, or maybe even educate them to more enlightened behavior? What kind of world are you creating?

Above all, keep learning from your encounters. The beauty of activism is that it provides deep and valuable lessons, especially when we pause to reflect. *Was I assertive enough? Was I too compliant or too militant? Did I read my adversary accurately? Was my spirit balanced in equipoise?* Take the time, and let the experience reverberate.

LIGHT ON YOUR FEET

The chains of habit are too weak to be felt until they are too strong to be broken.

Samuel Johnson

In the world of conflict and activism, surprises are inevitable. You can do all the homework you want, but there's no escaping the unknown. You can scout the opposition, learn their inclinations, imagine their motivations, and generate predictions about their next moves, but no matter how thorough your preparations, no matter how diligent your study, you may still be working in the dark.

And in fact, it's even worse than that. Deep, methodical preparation might actually make you *more* vulnerable than before. Intensive preparation takes time, and that means you're going to feel the commitment and burden of sunk costs. You've invested heavily in your project, and you're becoming increasingly committed to whatever it is you're doing. In the process, your imagination begins to congeal and close off your attention to novelty. As the Zen masters have taught, "In the beginner's mind are many possibilities, in the expert's there are few." In this sense, more may actually be less.

UPS AND DOWNS OF NEUROPLASTICITY

Like it or not, the butterfly world of activism is a world of uncertainty. You can plan, study, and train all you like, but, ultimately, you're going to have to show up with your body, your mind, your spirit, and your beliefs. And, you've got to be ready for anything.

No matter the issue or domain, our activism always seems to come down to a simple duality: We need the strength to prevail in conflict, but to remain effective in dynamic conditions, we've also got to be flexible. If you're too rigid, you're going to run into trouble, but if you're too compliant, you might well get run over by aggressors. All of which suggests a hybrid, athletic orientation for success: a dynamic balance of strong and flexible, hard and soft, and the willingness to change on the fly. In the world of high-performance skiing and snowboarding, this is known as being "tight-loose."

We see a similar idea in the world of modern athletic training where performance coaches sometimes ask their athletes a simple question: "Are you adapted or adaptable?" This, as it turns out, is a powerful koan for martial artistry, activism, and the art of living.

It's easy to see ups and downs in both directions. On the one hand, being highly *adapted* to a particular circumstance, setting, or challenge is a good thing. Disciplined practice increases your skill, your body transforms itself to meet conditions, and all goes well. But if conditions change, you may find yourself in real trouble. The skills, sensitivities, and capabilities you've worked so hard to establish may no longer be relevant, and they might even lead you in the wrong direction entirely.

Naturally, there's a neurological angle to all of this. When we practice and train for a particular challenge, the nervous system builds circuitry that's precisely and specifically appropriate to the conditions at hand. Every detail of synapses, nerve cells, and circuits becomes tightly wired to support the activity in question, whether it be athletics, music, scholarship, art, or craft.

The details go all the way down to the molecular level, and the process never really stops. In every minute of every day, your nervous system is creating extremely specific changes to support further instances of whatever it is you're trying to do. And each repetition solidifies your neural wiring. As they say in the world of neuroscience, "Cells that fire together, wire together." Or even better, "Circuits that fire together, wire together."

This neuroplasticity is a very good thing for anyone who wants to perform in a complex world. As soon as we enter a new situation, the body looks for patterns and starts the rewiring process. The more we repeat a behavior, the more the body responds, and the easier the behavior becomes. This process is very much akin to the growth of a watercourse in the mountains; one drop of water makes it easier for subsequent drops to follow the same path—thus the growth of creeks, rivers, valleys, and canyons.

THE TYRANNY OF HABIT

But the process is notoriously double-edged. The same neurological activity that gives us skill and adaptation also gives us habits of movement, sensation, cognition, and behavior, even habits of attitude and spirit. In turn, we bring these neural ruts and habitual inclinations to our conflicted encounters, engagements, and actions. No matter our best intentions, we're likely to do what we've always done. This is the shadow side of neuroplasticity.

But there's nothing to say that habits from one context will carry over to another. In fact, they might well lead us into awkwardness, poor performance, and tragic errors. If you're bringing your habitual inclinations into a new experiences, you'll be more vulnerable to novelty, surprise, and the bad behavior of your adversaries. You might be setting yourself up for catastrophe.

And thus our dilemma. As athletes and activists, we want our nervous systems to perform two very different tricks. On one hand, we want to create skillful, appropriate habits of sensation, movement, and behavior. On the other, we also want our neurological circuits to be fluid and malleable. In other words, we want to be *both* adapted and adaptable.

Obviously, much of this depends on your stage in life. Young people have yet to develop much in the way of habit and are less at risk for automated behavior in the face of change. But as the elders know, the older and deeper the habit, the harder it is to change. All of which points to a reversal of challenge as we get older. As children, we're quick to learn new ideas and behaviors, but as we age, the challenge is to unlearn and forget, to climb out of the neurological ruts that over-stabilize our behavior and put us at risk.

IMAGINE NO HABIT

So how do we revise the overlearned and overstabilized circuitry in our brains and bodies? How do we break free of our conditioning and our tendency to lapse back into the familiar? How do we become less adapted and more adaptable?

Be aware. A good first step is to understand and

acknowledge the nature of the challenge. Simply knowing the nature of neuroplasticity can go a long way towards avoiding the worst of the traps. Start by being skeptical of your training, your conditioning, and your behavior. When entering a new encounter, remind yourself: *There's a good chance that I'm running on habit...I'm likely to do what I've already done before.* This is particularly the case when stress hits the fan in an activist encounter.

Work with a coach. Look for someone who lives outside your habitual patterns. Coaches serve a vital role because they can catch us in those watershed moments when we're about to fall back into habit. In essence, coaches keep us from stagnating in our established comfort zones and force us to stay creative.

Slow down. When we're scrambling for speed, we're far more likely to fall back into familiar patterns and well-developed neurobehavioral ruts. If we can pause, even for a moment, we create an opportunity to do something different. As Viktor Frankl put it in *Man's Search for Meaning*: "Between stimulus and response there is a space. In that space is our power to choose our response. In our response lies our growth and our freedom."

Buddhist writer Jack Kornfield said much the same thing: "In a moment of stopping, we break the spell between past result and automatic reaction. When we pause, we can notice the actual experience, the pain or pleasure, fear or excitement. In the stillness before our habits arise, we become free."

REMEMBER THIS...

The good news is that we are capable of all of this. Just

like any other mammal, we can be *both* adapted and adapt-able. The typical dog is super adapted to his yard and his home, but he's also highly adaptable if asked to live some-where else. Our most successful athletes, artists, and musi-cians show a similar meta-ability. Disciplined practice will give you the skills and adaptations you seek, but conscious attention and intentional action will keep you from falling back into the ruts, valleys, and canyons of behavior.

CREATE FORWARD

Life can only be understood backwards; but it must be lived forwards.

Søren Kierkegaard

The thing about fighting with other humans is that you never really know what they're going to do. People are unpredictable, and some are incredibly devious. Adversaries are innovators and some are extremely intelligent. Prior training will increase your odds of success, but if you really want to survive and thrive, you've got to be creative.

On the face of it, activism may well seem to have little or nothing to do with what we think of as creativity or art. We're accustomed to thinking that action is mostly about changing laws and policies, or about electing the right candidates to office. But in fact, creativity lies right at the center of what we're trying to do. To put it another way, martial artistry, activism, and art are perfect allies.

Unfortunately, the words *art* and *creativity* come with some heavy and highly distracting baggage. Modern people often think of art as nothing more than pretty pictures, and even worse, believe that art is only for special people who are somehow "gifted" or "creative." But these assumptions sabotage our efforts at their roots. Not only do these beliefs limit what we create, they also hamstring our ability to move society and culture. In fact, art and creativity are intrinsic to the human experience and are absolutely essential in our fight for a functional future.

It's no wonder that activists and artists share so much common ground, an alliance sometimes expressed in the word *artivism*. The writer M. K. Asante describes it this way:

> The artivist uses her artistic talents to fight and struggle against injustice and oppression—by any medium necessary. The artivist merges commitment to freedom and justice with the pen, the lens, the brush, the voice, the body, and the imagination. The artivist knows that *to make an observation is to have an obligation*.

LATERAL THINKING

In practice, creativity is an essential antidote to the binary, dualistic thinking that so often comes with conflict. Our opponents hit, so we hit back. They hate us, so we hate them. Before long, our minds begin to narrow, and we can only see two possibilities: victory or defeat, winning or losing. All of which limits our options and squeezes the creativity out of the process.

It's completely understandable, of course. We see a problem or an injustice in the world, and we're moved to resist it directly. We see a dysfunctional policy, organization, or idea, and we push back. This may well be necessary and even noble, but it's also important to stay flexible. Don't get locked into the binary trap of forward-backward, advance-retreat.

This is where it's helpful to think about the human body and the planes of physical movement. As physical therapists and athletic coaches teach us, *sagittal* is forward-back, *frontal* is left-right, and *transverse* is rotational. By analogy, the danger lies in sagittal consciousness, getting trapped in the assumption that the only strategic options available are advance or retreat. In contrast, our creativity lies in the frontal and transverse planes, with side-steps, rotations, circles, and even spirals.

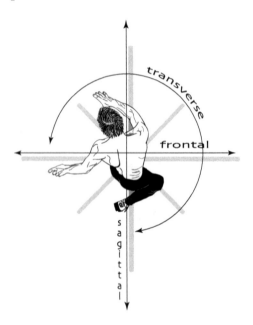

When attacked, sometimes the best course is to move your mind and spirit laterally to generate new options and possibilities. In the world of traditional martial arts, this is called "getting off the line" or, technically speaking, getting out of the sagittal plane. Your body is threatened by a kick or a punch, so you shift your position to the left or right without giving up your psychophysical integrity. You're not fleeing and you're not attacking; you're merely repositioning yourself to create new opportunities for movement.

The lesson, as always, is to keep your creative mobility alive. Don't get sucked into an adversarial mindset unless there are no other options. Don't allow your mind and spirit to be consumed or tyrannized by emotion and hatred. Stay out of the sagittal plane and stay alert for three-dimensional possibilities.

WORK-AROUNDS

It also helps to think in terms of work-arounds. A direct engagement might waste your time and energy, so why not create something completely different? This is the approach advocated by Buckminster Fuller, creator of tensegrity structures such as the geodesic dome. As Fuller saw it, "You never change things by fighting the existing reality. To change something, build a new model that makes the existing model obsolete." In other words, the martial artist creates *around* his enemy.

All of which gives us a fresh perspective. When we're being reactive and impulsive, it's easy to focus all our attention on the immediate threat. But with a creative work-around, you can almost ignore your adversary, at least for a time. You've got more important things to do; you're making something you believe in, something that has value in your eyes. And in this effort, you might even come to see your adversaries as less frightening; they're nothing more than noise in the system. To be sure, those adversaries may still matter, and it's wise to keep one eye on their behavior, but your opponents might turn out to be less of a threat than you imagined.

BRICOLAGE AND OPPORTUNISM

Closely related is the art of *bricolage,* using whatever's available to advance your creation. In this art, you don't worry much about styles, standard methods, best practices, or convention. Rather, you'll open your mind to possibility, innovation, and outrageous combination. As Bruce Lee put it in *Tao of Jeet Kune Do,* "Use only that which works, and take it from any place you can find it."

In conventional thinking, we're likely to suppose that our art has to look some particular way and that we've got to do our work in a particular settings and circumstances. We've got to be in a perfect studio with the right paints and brushes. We've got to have just the right musical instruments, the right computer software, the right tools, and the right materials. Everything has to be just so.

But why so fussy? Why limit your creativity to optimal conditions? The great cave artists of the Paleolithic era did amazing work using only natural materials like charcoal and pigments. They weren't waiting around for acrylics, airbrushes, or Photoshop to do their art. They looked around their habitat, experimented, and got to work.

Don't get distracted or tyrannized by optimal techniques, order, and above all, perfection. Work with whatever you've got on hand—allies, resources, ideas, or information. Don't get blocked by the fact that you don't have the right skills, the right materials, or the right training. Practice opportunism and seize the moments that come your way. Look around, see what you've got on hand, and get to it.

BEWARE THE BOX

Creativity also has a lot to teach us about the way we

organize or don't organize our thinking. You've probably noticed that as the world has become increasingly complex, people spend more and more of their time putting things in boxes—some of them real, but most of them conceptual. Overwhelmed by swarming, incessant tasks to be managed, we cope by sorting and organizing. All of which leads to a "boxification" of the modern world, and a rigid and sometimes violent pigeonholing of the human experience. In the process, we become constrained by our categories, and when something truly creative comes along, we don't know what to do with it.

And now, faced with an ecosocial crisis that doesn't fit into any historical box, many of the pigeonholes that we live by no longer serve us. In fact, they make genuine creativity extremely difficult. This is the tyranny of genre. Once you're in the box, your thinking will becomes compromised and your natural vagility constrained. You've been captured, incarcerated, hog-tied, maybe even domesticated. And once your efforts are rigidly defined, labeled, and categorized, your creativity is dead.

The conventional, inside-the-box advice is to "think outside the box." But the artivist goes much further and is skeptical of *all* pigeonholes, boilerplate language, templates, disciplinary boundaries, and any kind of ready-made forms that will boxify his or her efforts. So stop with the categories and go back to the world before words. Imagine no genres. As Bruce Lee famously described his martial philosophy, "One can function freely and totally if he is 'beyond system.' The man who is really serious, with the urge to find out what truth is, has no style at all. He lives only in what is."

CREATE FORWARD, HEAL FORWARD

Another obstacle to creative action is the fact that we're often looking in the wrong direction. Traumas big and small come into our lives, and we long to regain the sense of control, predictability, and wholeness that we experienced in days gone by. We tell our friends that we're going to "get back in shape," and we dream about returning to our former state of youthful vigor and exuberance. We imagine degraded ecosystems bouncing back to their original, old-growth glory after being raped by strip-mining, clear-cutting, and development. It's no wonder we see a growing industry of resilience training in education, business, community settings, and leadership. Everyone wants to go back.

But our thinking is flawed. The river of ecosystem function, physiology, and life only flows forward, and it's never the same river twice. Strictly speaking, there can be no bouncing back for any living systems, bodies, or habitats. Healing does occur, but when it does, it's always a transformation to some new state of integration. The thing we call "resilience" is really a creative process of moving forward.

Suppose you suffer an athletic injury. With rest and treatment, you'll probably get over it, and you might even come to the conclusion that you're "back to normal." But the tissue in question is different than before. Your body has engineered a work-around and some compensations—there's some scar tissue, some thickening of fibers, maybe some new neural stimulation to your muscular system. Your body works well enough now and it no longer gives you pain, but in essence, it's really a different body. You haven't bounced back; *you've bounced forward.*

The same holds true for habitat. When a forest ecosystem burns or is clear-cut, it eventually transforms to a new state of function and health. We might say that it heals, but conditions are not precisely the same. Some species have disappeared and new ones have taken hold. Given enough time, the forest grows again and may even appear to have recovered, but there are subtle new relationships between plants, animals, and microorganisms.

The problem with our popular image of resilience is that it offers a false hope of return. We lead ourselves to believe we can rebound to a golden age when everything was working or "as nature intended." All our modern "re" words suffer a similar flaw: *return, restore, rebound, rebuild, rewild, regenerate, recuperate.* The belief is seductive: with good luck and hard work, we can take the broken pieces, repair them, and put them back into their original order, and everything will be "as good as new." But this belief in retro-resilience can blind us to the very actions we need to move forward. Even worse, it can leave us feeling hopeless—if going back seems impossible, then there's nothing left but to suffer.

This orientation towards "healing forward" and "creating forward" might sound like a strategy for occasional use, especially in the wake of trauma, injury, or disease. But when we take the lesson to heart, we start looking at our lives from a whole new perspective. In this, creating and healing forward become fundamental skills in their own right. This is not just something we do in the aftermath of an adverse events; it's an orientation we can practice every day, always working with what we've got on hand, continuously putting together new combinations that move us ahead. In this practice, healing and creating forward are muscles that get stronger with use.

GET OVER IT...

Ultimately, the path to creativity consists mostly of getting out of our own way, in letting go of the blocks, the obstacles, and the assumptions of powerlessness that drag us down. Ignore the creativity-killing obstacles of the modern world, and you'll be left with the raw, essential experience you're looking for. Above all, get over the belief that art has to look a certain way or that it's only for special people. Creativity is a human universal; everyone can do something. Everyone *must* do something.

EXTRAORDINARY FORCES

I feel an indescribable ecstasy and delirium in melting, as it were, into the system of being, in identifying myself with the whole of nature.

Jean-Jacques Rousseau

The battle for the earth is asymmetrical, frustrating, and exhausting. The enemy is wickedly strong, grossly overpowered, and often ruthless. Anti-future forces are massively entrenched, have deep pockets, and are heavily defended—legally, politically, and culturally. In contrast, pro-future forces are woefully underfunded, lack political power, and are often marginalized.

So it's no wonder that the activist often feels worn down and burned out. Climate fatigue, compassion fatigue, hope fatigue—these are common afflictions for anyone who's trying to make a difference. We work hard, do our homework, and stick our necks out, but nothing seems to change. Even worse, we often feel isolated. Activism can be lonely work, and it sometimes feels like we're surrounded by millions of people who don't care and can't be bothered. It's no wonder we feel so frazzled.

The good news is that robust vitality is possible. In his great classic *The Art of War*, Sun Tzu wrote about the interplay of the "normal and extraordinary forces" that move great armies on the battlefield. His original thinking has been lost to history, but for our purposes, nature is the ultimate extraordinary force, the awesome power that flows through habitat and our bodies in every minute of every day. This is the unified force of biology, ancestry, plants, animals, and wildness. If we can feel and harness this vitality, we'll be more powerful, robust, and effective.

BLINDNESS AND DYSFUNCTION

Sadly and tragically, a substantial majority of modern people are effectively out of touch with these extraordinary forces—stranded, alienated, and adrift. Writing in the mid-twentieth century, psychologist Carl Jung put it this way: "Man feels himself isolated in the cosmos. He is no longer involved in nature and has lost his emotional participation in natural events."

Jung saw our situation clearly. In decades gone by, people came in routine contact with robust, exuberant life in wild areas and even in cities on occasion. People were never far from mammals, birds, insects, and other creatures, all of whom stood as physical reminders of the extraordinary powers of life. But today, such contact is rare, and it's no wonder that so many of us are suffering from psychophysical ailments and the quagmire of depression, anxiety, and alienation.

We are blinded in many ways, most obviously by the layers of insulation that now surround our bodies. Airtight houses and workplaces, near-perfect clothing, and hermetically sealed vehicles literally keep us out of touch with the living world. We've become massively insulated animals, separated from the extraordinary forces by layer upon layer of plastic, concrete, miracle fabrics, and engineered glass. We scarcely touch anything at all, much less the tissue of the living world.

As children, we many of us were in intimate, daily contact with the extraordinary forces of the natural world. The night sky, the ocean, and the textures, sounds, and sensations of life filled our bodies and imaginations with energy; the experience was immediate, powerful, and, for many of us, extremely influential. But over time, we grew accustomed to these experiences, and after a few decades, some of us even lost touch with them entirely. In this sense, modern humans are like superheroes with a bad case of amnesia. Our bodies are literally saturated with power, but we've forgotten how to feel and harness it.

We're also seduced and distracted by our many inventions. As modern people, we're quick to leapfrog over the primal systems of life and go directly to the fancy, artificial wonders. Unable to feel our intrinsic powers, we look to technologies, fossil fuels, computers, and devices in the hope that some of their power will rub off on us. We're so in awe of our creations that we fail to see the ancient and incredibly sophisticated capability that's flowing through our bodies and our lives.

This is the displacement cost of modern civilization. Say what you will about the practical benefits of modern inventions, the fact remains that they also distract us from the primal, extraordinary forces of life. For every hour we spend watching and listening to the products of the civilized world, that's an hour we're *not* spending in contact with the living planet. Taken in total, this amounts to the displacement of billions of hours of human attention each year.

To take a cosmic perspective, if an alien power had come to Earth and systematically distracted human attention away from our life-supporting systems, we would surely have considered it an intentional criminal act—an attentional crime of immense proportions—even an act of war. This alienation from the extraordinary forces of the natural world—completely apart from our ecological crisis—should be seen as a psycho-spiritual catastrophe in its own right.

WAKING UP TO THE EXTRAORDINARY

If you're young, you still have one foot in the world of extraordinary power, and it's easy to remember the feeling of outrageous physicality, creativity, and wildness. But if you're a grown adult, you might be suffering some degree of amnesia. The good news is that it's all there for the taking and none of it is any great secret: Spend more time outside, reestablish circadian harmony by avoiding artificial light, pay more attention to habitat, and weave yourself back into the world.

The common prescription holds that we should engage in vigorous, outdoor physical movement, sometimes called "exercise." When we move our bodies outdoors, we participate in a process that's as old as evolution, an experience that's common to all life on this planet. When we move in natural settings, our bodies become more permeable to sensation and the outrageous vitality that flows through habitat, plants, and animals.

But the essence of this practice isn't really the physical exercise itself; it's our exposure and vulnerability to the natural world. This is why it's so important to unplug and free yourself from digital distraction. When going for a hike, leave your phone behind. Your device may seem innocent, but the attentional consequences are severe. By fragmenting your awareness, the device actually weakens your connection to the extraordinary forces. Any psycho-spiritual or health benefits you might actually gain from your outdoor activity will be compromised, if not completely extinguished.

In general, the best practice is to go *towards* outdoor exposure and vulnerability. Yes, being safe in the outdoors is important, and if you're genuinely afraid of remote wilderness, carrying a device might be prudent. But if you really want to feel the extraordinary forces, you've got to get outside your comfort zone. This means going into unfamiliar territory and taking on the elements. It means embracing the discomfort, carrying a heavy pack, going higher on the mountain, deeper into the wilderness, into the hot and the cold. If you want to feel the extraordinary forces, you're going to have to work for it.

This would also be a good time to think about language. When going outdoors into natural places, the way we choose to talk makes a big difference in the quality of our experience; the words we speak will either reinforce or diminish our contact with the extraordinary forces. This suggests a discipline for our outdoor adventures. That is, keep your voice down and limit your conversation to living the things, especially those that you see around you: plants, animals, soil, water, light, weather, and people. Avoid conversation about civilized subjects like work, technology, news, media, politics, and money. You'll have plenty of time to talk about these distractions when you get back to the city.

KEEP YOUR EYE ON THE AWE

The extraordinary forces are all around us and inside us, but, sadly, we often fall asleep to their power, lulled into complacency by familiarity. We've lived for decades with these forces, and with each passing day, they fade from consciousness and may even disappear from awareness entirely. If we could feel even a fraction of the immensity of ancestry and biology that surrounds us, we'd be energized beyond belief.

In our historically normal, Paleolithic world, awe was commonplace. The human mind and body were in constant contact with the magnificence and enormity of nature. Thunderstorms, lightning displays, and wildfires were daily events. Animal dramas played out in real time, right before our ancestors' eyes. With no light pollution whatsoever, the night sky would have blazed with an intensity modern humans can scarcely imagine. And around a tribe's local habitat, vast reaches of unknown territory stretched to the horizon, home to whatever our imagination might conjure. On most days, nature filled our ancestors with radical amazement. In other words, awe was a consistent, normal feature of life—a human universal.

So perhaps it's no surprise to learn that modern scientists have confirmed the benefits of this primal experience. Research has shown that people who watched a nature video that elicited awe were subsequently more ethical, more generous, and described themselves as being more connected to others—qualities that are commonplace in indigenous traditions.

Awe makes people happier and less stressed, even weeks later. It assists the immune system by dampening the production of inflammatory cytokines. Awe activates the parasympathetic nervous system, which works to calm the fight-or-flight response. It gives people a greater sense of time and helps us break out of habitual thinking patterns.

There's a prosocial benefit as well. Researchers have argued that awe is the ultimate collective emotion because it motivates people to do things that enhance the greater good. Awe shifts our focus from narrow self-interest to the welfare of the tribe. It helps bind us to others, motivating us to act in collaborative ways that enable strong groups and cohesive communities. Which, of course, is an ideal quality for people in both ancestral and modern life.

BE SMALL TO BE POWERFUL

Awe is out there, wrapping the planet in a full-time embrace of beauty, energy, and complexity. We'd like to feel it, but we're blinded by our hubris and our belief in human supremacy. As our power over the natural world has grown, our sense of self-importance and species-level narcissism has also become more pronounced. Today, many of us are inclined to see ourselves as giants, as designers of the future, and as saviors of the planet. We tend to believe that *we* are the extraordinary force on this planet and that nature is little more than a supporting cast, a bit player in our exclusively human drama.

The solution, as the elders would surely remind us, is humility. In other words, if you really want to feel the power of the natural world, it's best to shrink your profile and start participating with natural processes. As the deep ecologist Arne Næss put it, "The smaller we come to feel ourselves compared to the mountain, the nearer we come to participating in its greatness."

This sheds new light on human behavior in an ecological context. In the popular imagination, we're quick to reject low-impact lifestyle solutions because they seem to diminish our profile and importance in the world. Austerity and simplicity strike us as unacceptable; we fear the prospect of becoming lesser beings. But we fail to see the existential and psycho-spiritual upside. That is, by reducing our energy consumption and living a more modest existence, we've got a better shot at actually participating in and feeling the immensity of the living world. By stepping down from our self-declared pedestal of superiority, we actually become stronger. In this sense, being small is the path to real greatness.

REMEMBER THIS...

There's power all around you and inside you, so don't fall asleep. Feel it with your beginner's body and remember what was really there all along. Even if you're stuck in the city, look for evidence of ancient life in trees, water, sky, wind, and rain. Reflect on the habitat, plants, and animals that give you food and life. Read about biology and, above all, the immensely powerful history of life on this planet. These experiences may seem modest, but they will sustain you through the big challenges ahead. As Sun Tzu put it in *The Art of War*, "The resources of those skilled in the use of extraordinary forces are as infinite as the heavens and earth; as inexhaustible as the flow of the great rivers."

RHYTHM, PACE, AND TIMING

Trust only movement. Life happens at the level of events, not of words. Trust movement.

Alfred Adler

Austrian psychotherapist, 1870–1937

The Greek philosopher Heraclitus had it right: we just can't step into the same river twice. Every last plant, animal, and microorganism on the planet is in motion. People and relationships are in constant flux, with shifting values, perspectives, priorities, and behaviors. Our adversaries are always maneuvering, and even our allies are changing. The action that worked yesterday may well have an entirely different effect and meaning tomorrow. If we're going to be successful as martial artists and activists, we've got to understand and appreciate the nature of movement.

But, sadly, our modern world has very little sense of natural motion, or to be more precise, it has only one sense of motion—linear, sagittal speed. Faster is always better. The way to get ahead is to step it up, be productive, and keep pushing. A vast array of ever-faster products, services, and training programs are standing by to help us push the pace. Slowing down is not even on our radar.

All of which is profoundly out of step with the natural behavior and function of living systems. Children and nonhuman animals see this clearly, as did our Paleolithic ancestors. Daylight waxes and wanes, seasons come and go.

There's a time for hunting and a time for rest. There's a time to accelerate and there's a time to lie low.

PACE

The first priority for the activist is to regain some sense of natural time and pace. Move in harmony with the world, and you're more likely to feel the extraordinary forces at work. Move at the pace of habitat, and your body and mind will simply work better. In turn, you'll have more energy to bring to the challenges and activism in your life.

It's a simple ask, and yet, it feels almost impossible for most of us. That's because we live in a world of perverse incentives which is to say, there are myriad forces in culture and society that push us to push the pace. The promotion of speed is all around us now, and the sense of urgency is contagious. Growing up in such a system literally changes the tissues of our bodies and our brains; our nervous systems are now wired for an ever-present anxiety that calls out for yet more speed.

But the cure for speed addiction takes time, and it feels unsettling. For many of us, sitting still may feel like the most challenging thing in the world, but remember, the sense of urgency that you're feeling may well be artificial and completely unnecessary. You're feeling anxious not because of any particular demand or a flaw in your personality, but because you've been duped. Modern media and advertising have pumped up your sense of urgency to a fever pitch, and now you can barely sit still. So, it's not you; it's the world you're living in. Let go of the perverse incentives, and you'll naturally slow down.

METABOLIZE YOUR EXPERIENCE

Things happen. Surprises disrupt our days and our expectations, people come and go, and relationships fall apart, sometimes without warning. Unpleasant jolts, traumas, and inexplicable behaviors upset our equanimity and send our minds reeling. On some days, we're lucky to function at all.

If this was a prehistoric Paleolithic world, we'd know exactly what to do: slow down, sit down, or wander off to the perimeter of camp where we could let it all sink in or fade away. We'd absorb the experience, turn it over a few times, and then, when the time was right, rejoin our friends and family. But the modern world allows for none of these things. We're expected to shake off traumas and disasters in an instant so we can get back into action and above all, productivity.

But there can be no pushing the pace on these life experiences. The body needs time to metabolize challenges, to reframe and reintegrate the disruptions; we need time to gather our wits. Without this interval, we have no choice but to suppress our experience and drive it down into some deep psychic pigeonhole, where it might well reemerge at the worst possible moment.

The cure, as always, is attention. Honor the surprises, the novel experiences, and the stressful events, and let your body take care of itself. Let the experiences settle into your tissue and your life. Take all the time you need. Breathe, relax, and let it be.

RHYTHM

Looking at the state of the modern world, what we see

is something that seems very much like a chronic disease, a relentless assault on our life-supporting systems and, in turn, our spirits. In every minute of every day, massive amounts of carbon are being pumped into the atmosphere. In every minute of every day, species are being forced out of their homes, oceans are being over-fished, forests are being cut down, soil and groundwater are being depleted, mountaintops are being "removed," and minerals are being strip-mined. The destruction never stops.

All of which is not just depressing, it but also poses a massive challenge for the health and sanity of the activist. When we realize the chronic nature of the destruction, we're tempted to answer with our own chronic efforts. If the destruction never stops, neither should we, so we double down and triple down on our efforts. Nothing is ever enough, so we work harder. More meetings, more homework, more actions, more time at the keyboard. We triage out the nonessentials and devote ever more energy to the fight.

But, of course, all this chronic striving is destined to fail or even make things worse. Hard work is obviously essential and honorable, but to remain effective, the human animal has to keep a beat. In fact, our entire biological history is built around oscillating patterns of engagement and rest. In their 1988 book *The Paleolithic Prescription*, anthropologists S. Boyd Eaton, Marjorie Shostak, and Melvin Konner described an oscillating pattern of hunting and resting in native people as "the Paleolithic rhythm."

Without question, this pattern of serious exertion and deep rest is the norm for human beings. Even well into the age of agriculture, natural light ruled human activity, and people lived a rhythmic lifestyle. There can be no question that this kind of oscillation kept us strong and resilient.

For the activist, this understanding poses a challenge and a lesson. Yes, our predicament is a genuine emergency that demands radical action and sustained, even desperate effort. And yes, it's hard to relax when you know the devastation that's going on just outside your door. But it's also true that you've got to keep your strength up. You won't be of much use to anyone if you burn up your body and spirit with chronic engagement. On the contrary, you'll flame out and lapse back into the quagmire of exhaustion, depression, and despair. Every athletic coach knows how this works: intensive training must always oscillate with deep rest. Otherwise, the effort is wasted.

All of which argues for a high-contrast lifestyle of engagement and down time. Fight the fight as best you can, then allow the animal to heal up. Engage your adversary, then retreat to a safe haven. Focus as intensely as possible, then give your time and attention over to deep relaxation. For the passionate and committed activist, this may be the greatest challenge of all, but it remains essential.

TIMING

Rhythm is vital, but it's also important for the activist to act at the opportune moment. When you get the timing right, the process is easy and you're likely to be effective, but if you get it wrong, you'll have to work harder or, worse yet, suffer the collapse of your entire effort.

This is why it's good practice to show up early, a strategy that's long been recognized by elders in a variety of cultures. Sun Tzu put it this way in *The Art of War*: "He who excels at resolving difficulties does so before they arise.

He who excels in conquering his enemies triumphs before threats materialize."

In the *Tao te Ching*, Lao Tzu wrote:

> It is easy to maintain a situation while it is still secure. It is easy to deal with a situation before symptoms develop; It it is easy to break a thing when it is yet brittle; It it is easy to dissolve a thing when it is yet minute. Deal with a thing while it is still nothing; keep a thing in order before disorder sets in.

Even Shakespeare had a similar understanding: "Meet the first beginnings; look to the budding mischief before it has time to ripen to maturity." Or, as a Cherokee parable so vividly puts it, "Pay attention to the whispers so you don't have to listen to the screams." In other words, be assertive in taking on the microbattles and the incipient conflicts at their roots. Act early and upstream, before the momentum takes over.

EQUIPOISE

All of which makes good sense, but it also presents the martial artist with a dilemma: On one hand, the elders tell us to act early, but on the other, they also counsel forbearance and patience. As Sun Tzu himself put it, "The wise warrior avoids the battle. . . . If you wait by the river long enough, the bodies of your enemies will float by." And, "He who is prudent and lies in wait for an enemy who is not, will be victorious." So which is it? Shall we act early and decisively or let things take care of themselves?

There can be no ultimate answer, and for the activist, it

will always be a judgment call. What works in one circumstance might well fail in another. What succeeds against one opponent might well antagonize another. The martial artistry is to embrace it all in equipoise. In other words, hold both potentials together in a single state of mind and spirit.

REMEMBER THIS...

Ultimately, the body itself gives us a powerful metaphor for intelligent action. When faced with the challenge of competing demands, think and move like an athlete: be both strong and flexible, powerful and adaptable, tight and loose. Don't get trapped into an either-or mindset, body-set, or spirit-set. Be capable of spontaneous action and revision. Don't over-commit to any particular strategy of engagement, unless and until the moment demands it. Instead, maintain a both-and sensibility and a strong-fluid capability, guided by sensation and experience.

In the end, the right timing will come from your attention, awareness, diligence, and understanding. Listen to the wind and you'll move in harmony with the world.

ALLIES AND ADVERSARIES

I would rather walk with a friend in the dark, than alone in the light.

Helen Keller

Standing alone in the wilderness is a scary, often dangerous proposition. Whether you're out on the open grassland of prehistory or on some kind of modern activist battleground, it's always a good idea to circle up. A few good allies will reduce your exposure and limit your vulnerability. This understanding lives deep in our evolutionary history, in the circuits of our brains and our bodies.

But strangely, we rarely give much thought to the matter. In fact, we often choose our allies impulsively, even at random. We affiliate with some people and oppose others by habit, by tradition, by appearance and feel, or simply by convenience. Even worse, these affiliations may have nothing to do with our personal values and sense of meaning. And it's not much help to have allies who don't really believe in what you're doing.

So before you begin sorting out your allies and adversaries, there's one fundamental fact of human behavior, society, and politics that you must remember: *conditions, alliances, and opponents are going to change.* For better and for worse, people and their relationships are always in flux. Today's allies might defect; today's adversaries might well become tomorrow's supporters.

IS MY WORLD FRIENDLY?

The problem is that most of us are quick to sort the people into two camps. Instantly and unconsciously, we label the people around us as *with us* or *against us*. And it's astonishing how often we actually go out of our way to seek out and create opposition, sometimes out of thin air. People irritate us, but we're not sure why. Their facial expressions, postures, mannerisms, and tones of voice grate on our nerves, so we fire up our resistance. Operating on impulse, we project our anxieties onto others and jump into battles that don't even need to be fought. Stressed and anxious, we just want to fight *something*.

From a deep and prehistoric perspective, these impulsive judgment calls might make some sense, and there's probably some evolutionary advantage that goes to those who make quick judgment calls about tribal and personal affiliation. Our inclinations towards or away from people are shaped in large measure by our personal history and the autonomic nervous system, the deep ancient wiring that regulates the basic functions of the entire body. We've all heard about the two branches: one moves the body towards action—the *fight-flight* response—while the other moves us towards *rest-and-digest*, the so-called *feed-and-breed* response.

In every moment of every day, the autonomic nervous system is asking a basic survival question: *"Is my world friendly?"* If the answer is "yes," the rest-and-digest branch of the autonomic system kicks in, and, in turn, we approach the world with a greater sense of openness, curiosity, and tolerance. When we meet a stranger, we're more likely to suppose that this person is a potential ally, a friend in the making. But if the answer is "no," we're more vigilant and skeptical. Meet meet the very same stranger on the street, and we're more likely to imagine him as a potential adversary, an enemy at large.

MAKE NO UNNECESSARY ENEMIES

The lesson is that we're almost never objective. Most of the time, it's the body that's calling the shots, and we can be wildly wrong about a person's true nature. This argues for caution and introspection:

> Is my assessment of this person or group based on reality or on the fact that I'm really stressed today?

> Is my personal history of trauma coloring my view?

> Am I pigeonholing this person or group by impulse, or am I making a reasoned evaluation of their character, stance, and motives?

All of which leads us to a simple set of general principles for martial artistry and living: Don't be in such a hurry to define people and groups as opponents. Don't make assumptions, and don't go looking for trouble. Feel what you're feeling, but reserve judgment as long as possible. Above all, make no unnecessary enemies. The person or group that looks most threatening might well be your greatest ally in days to come.

DO I FEEL FELT?

To really understand our relationships with allies and adversaries, it's essential that we consider a the fundamental social needs of the human animal. The good news is that it's really quite simple: No matter our background, history, or culture, all of us have a deep-seated desire to feel seen, heard, felt, understood, and respected. This is a human universal; people of every age, culture, origin, and status crave this experience. Even the Na'vi, the fictional indigenous people of Pandora depicted in the movie *Avatar*, address one another with the honorific "I see you."

This social need is far more than a superficial, emotional desire. It's rock-solid biology that goes all the way to the deepest levels of physiology and nervous system function, as real as our need for food and water. When the body feels recognized and appreciated, we feel safe; in turn, the autonomic nervous system goes into action, repairing tissues and opening up the aperture of cognition and creativity. Without question, the experience of being recognized is a powerful and inexpensive form of medicine in its own right.

The trick is time. The people around us want to feel felt, heard, seen, understood, and respected, but the process requires focused, sincere attention—something that's in short supply in our hyperactive world. In fact, our modern rush for speed doesn't just give us stress, it radically undermines the human connections that we would otherwise have with one another. When everyone's in a rush, no one is going to feel felt. And when no one feels felt, people become afraid, suspicious and vigilant. This is why digital "communication" is so corrosive; when words are moving at the speed of light, the vital experience of feeling felt fades away, and we're left with nothing but a handful of ghostly bits and bytes.

Obviously, it makes sense to treat our allies with sincere

attention and see to it that they feel felt, but it's just as important to give a similar experience to our adversaries and opponents. Everyone's human; everyone wants to feel felt, seen, heard, respected, and understood. You may not like the person across the table, and you might well loathe their policies, their values, and their behavior, but authentic attention costs very little and can go a long way towards creative resolution, or at least a continued negotiation.

This is where we so often sabotage ourselves. Acting on impulse, we pay sincere and sustained attention to the people we feel comfortable with, but snub those who make us feel anxious. In the process, we actually create adversaries out of thin air and alienate those who might actually become allies. The people in question don't feel felt, seen, heard, or respected, and in turn, go looking for any excuse to thwart our interests in the future. They may not remember precisely what you said in the past, but they'll be sure to remember how they felt in your presence.

And remember, this orientation has nothing to do with capitulation or passive acceptance of your adversary's position. You might well disagree with everything your opponents says and stands for, but you can still make that person feel felt. You might well reject his arguments, positions, values and ideology, but you can still give him the experience of feeling understood and respected. In other words, you can help him "save face." It may be a heavy lift to give your adversaries this sense of recognition, but it's solid martial artistry. If your opponents feel seen and respected in their encounters with you, there's a better chance that they'll move in your direction, or at least remember you as a good human.

TREAT EVERYONE LIKE A POTENTIAL ALLY

In a world of constantly shifting alliances and butterfly effects, even the most perceptive martial artist will remain largely ignorant of how human relationships and coalitions will play out. And given this fundamental uncertainty, the best practice is to treat everyone you meet like a potential ally. Honor your ignorance and the fundamentally dynamic nature of human relationships. No matter how smart you might be, there's no way to predict the flux and flow of human alliances; people are always breaking up and making up. The people you meet might well seem misinformed, superficial, ignorant, or woefully misguided on vital issues, but all of that can change in a heartbeat. Play a long game; don't close doors unless there's no alternative.

CHOOSE A GOOD ALLY

As we've seen, it's tempting to simply gang up with whoever makes us feel comfortable and oppose whoever makes us feel uneasy. We humans are quick to join forces with those who look familiar and to resist those who look or sound different from what we're used to. But this is a perilous trap. Allies and adversaries come to us from surprising directions, and they rarely behave according to our expectations. Even when people differ about on the details of your issue, you'll want to keep them in your sights; you might want to form a coalition later on.

In any case, the way you feel around potential allies matters a great deal. Do these people make you feel felt, heard, seen, understood, and respected? If the answer is yes, you're off to a good start. Your potential allies are listening and, paying attention, and they might even care about who you are. There's a good chance that you can work together.

This also tells you something important about the really crucial issue: how these potential allies might behave in a crisis. If this person or group has a track record of listening and paying attention, there's a good chance that they'll perform well when chaos hits the fan.

REMEMBER THIS...

In the long run, appearances tell us little, if anything, of importance. What really matters is character. Will this person stand up when chaos strikes? Do they demonstrate integrity in speech and action? Do they take responsibility? Are they curious about the world? Are they willing to take risks? To be sure, these questions won't give you a complete picture of potential allies, but it's a very a good place to start.

LOVE AND RAGE

Being an ecologist in 2022 is like being a scholar in the Library of Alexandria while it burns. At some point, you put down the books and pick up a fire hose. We do this work because we love it, and we can't bear to see it destroyed.

Activist, Scientist Rebellion

Who or what do you identify with? What makes you who you are? For the vast majority of human history, the answer to this question was clear. People felt a powerful affiliation with the land around them, a life-supporting system that gave them not just food and water, but also a sense of beauty and awe. It's no wonder that so many native people say, "I am the land, the land is me," "I am the forest, the forest is me," "I am the river, the river is me." For indigenous people, the body and the land are not just connected, they are continuous.

But for modern people, such identification is a hit-or-miss proposition. Many of us have no significant relationship with habitat, and even for people who do spend time outdoors, much of that time is recreational, athletic, or simply an escape from the mentally exhausting confines of city life. Nevertheless, some of us do manage to connect to something deeper. Maybe we have an outdoor experience that feels particularly powerful and engaging. We feel a sense of intimacy and identification with the plants, animals, water, and soils of the earth, and in the process, we experience nature as a literal extension of our bodies. This is what biologist E. O. Wilson called *biophilia*, our innate desire to affiliate with the natural world.

So far, so good. But the next step is what really shakes things up. Suddenly, we start to see the destruction of the biosphere in a new light. In his great classic *A Sand County Almanac*, author Aldo Leopold noted that "one of the penalties of an ecological education is that one lives alone in the world of wounds." And the more we identify with nature, the more it hurts.

The exploitation of habitat, road building, fossil fuel projects, mining, and industrial agriculture—these practices aren't just ugly and unsustainable—they are literally forms of violence against the planet, future generations, and the tissue of our own bodies. All of which leads inexorably to a potent sense of anger and outrage. How can we be so insane, so suicidal, so destructive to this most precious of all beings, the life that literally keeps us alive?

All of which makes us wonder about the kind of spirit we should bring to our activism. Should our efforts be based on our love for the natural world, or should we act with outrage at its destruction? And what if appeals to nature's beauty and magnificence fall on deaf ears? Should we turn up the heat and rage against the machine?

A HYBRID APPROACH

It's easy to see problems in both directions. Our love of the living world is powerful, but in a world that plays hardball politics, it's unlikely to move the needle on important issues. It's an unfortunate fact that people in power are often unmoved by anything other than power itself. But anger can be alienating and counterproductive. By itself, anger is generally not a good way to persuade people, nurture allies, or turn adversaries in your direction.

So wisdom would suggest a hybrid approach, equal parts passion and outrage. We start with love, our original motivation for defending the living world. We see ourselves as protectors and defenders of something sacred, something vital. In this role, we're taking action as warriors—in the traditional, native sense of the word.

In recent years, we've heard a good deal of talk about the "warrior spirit" and references to wildlife warriors, solar warriors, spiritual warriors, warrior activists, and a thousand other variations on the theme. But if we really want to get to the root, we have to remember that the original meaning of the warrior ethic is sacrifice for others, including habitat, tribe, and community. The English writer G. K. Chesterton said it best: "A true warrior fights not because he hates what's in front of him, but because he loves what's behind him."

SACRED RAGE

But love is only half of the whole; we've also got to bring our anger, our discontent, and outrage to the table. The problem is that we've been told that anger is a problem. If you've been conditioned by modern culture, you might even be tempted to lie about your feelings. You might choose to present yourself as a calm person, of even temper, filled with grace and equanimity. Anger is dangerous, we're told, and it's best to keep it under wraps. We're expected to suppress it, dampen it, manage it, control it. You might even be ashamed of your anger and claim that it doesn't really exist.

Prevailing cultural belief holds that anger is a personality flaw, even a neuropsychiatric disorder. If you're angry, there's something wrong with you that needs to be managed and dampened by practice and self-control. If you're angry, you need an anger-management course, therapy, and/or medication. In particular, you need a more powerful pre-frontal cortex to bring all that nastiness under strict neurological control. If your hair is on fire, you need to put the fire out.

But what if anger is a normal, healthy human-animal response to abnormal circumstances and a chaotic, alien environment? What if your anger is an appropriate, rational, life-affirming response to the destruction of life-supporting habitat? What if your anger is fundamentally rational? And what if the *absence* of anger is the real the dysfunction of our age?

Indeed, research suggests that "eco-anger" is actually a powerfully functional emotion. In 2021, the *Journal of Climate Change and Health* found that

> ...experiencing eco-anger predicted better mental
> health outcomes, as well as greater engagement
> in pro-climate activism and personal behaviours.
> Eco-anxiety and eco-depression were less adaptive,
> relating to lower wellbeing... Our findings
> implicate anger as a key adaptive emotional driver of
> engagement with the climate crisis...

In other words, if you're furious, you may well be on the right track. Given the violence now being inflicted upon the earth, anger is really a marker of attention, awareness, and continuity with the biosphere. As we've seen, the historically normal, indigenous worldview sees the body and habitat as continuous and part of a single whole. From this perspective, the destruction of habitat is very much akin to an attack on our very tissue. As Australian aboriginal elders have put it, "To wound the earth is to wound yourself, and if others are wounding the earth, they are wounding you."

So isn't your anger the sign of a healthy, wild animal fighting back against the destruction of its habitat? Doesn't it make sense that an increasing number of street-level protests signs declare "We are nature defending herself"? Wouldn't the absence of anger signal a dysfunction in the human animal? This is precisely why Native American activist John Trudell once warned, "Don't trust anyone who isn't angry."

Anger is a reflection of our values, our attention, and a healthy concern for what we hold dear. As Edward Abbey put it, "Love implies anger. The man who is angered by nothing cares about nothing." And if you love habitat—as historically normal humans do—then you ought to be furious. People sometimes ask, "Why are you so angry?" but in the context of rampant habitat destruction around the world, the appropriate response is, "Why are you not?"

PRECISION RAGE

To be sure, the anger can burn too hot, and it's easy to work ourselves into a state of rage intoxication; in this state, things can go sideways in a hurry. Yes, some forms of anger are dysfunctional, and to be sure, a broad-spectrum, unfocused anger that randomly erupts is definitely counterproductive. But what's lost in the conversation is the fact that the absence of anger is a signal of something gone horribly wrong: exhaustion, capitulation, resignation, apathy, domestication, or denial.

The trick is to focus our anger, to channel it, clarify it, and above all, make it functional. Random acts of rage are worthless, but precision anger is precious. In other words, stop being triggered over minor upsets, trivial issues, and superficial annoyances. Instead, be angry about the alpha issues of our time, the megafaunal threats to our habitats, our bodies, our democracy, and the planet as a whole. Be angry about the fact that your future is being chopped up and sold off to whoever's willing to pay.

To paraphrase a famous passage from the Greek philosopher Aristotle: "the goal is to be angry with the right thing, to the right degree, at the right time, for the right purpose, and in the right way." It won't be much help to be angry with the entire human species, or the totality of the modern world, but it might be useful to be angry with the cultural narratives of "man over nature" or "profit over planet." And it might be even more useful to be angry with specific policies, organizations, and programs that destroy habitat and, in turn, our future.

REMEMBER...

Our anger and rage are healthy expressions of our animal nature and our fight for life. Even our anxiety, depression, doubt, and confusion are sacred. As the ecotherapist Joanna Macy put it, "The sorrow, grief, and rage you feel is a measure of your humanity and your evolutionary maturity."

So don't suppress your emotion; channel it. Care for your anger and give it the respect it deserves. Focus it to a laser point and remember: there's nothing wrong with you. On the contrary, there's something very much right with you. Now, more than ever, we need that energy.

ACTIVISM IS MEDICINE

Life is not an easy matter. You cannot live through it
without falling into frustration and cynicism unless
you have before you a great idea which raises you
above personal misery, above weakness, above all
kinds of perfidy and baseness.

Leon Trotsky

Marxist revolutionary, 1879–1940

In the popular imagination, activism is usually seen as
an outward-facing, external enterprise. It's about creating change; it's about doing things in the world and to
the world. But what if activism is even bigger than all that?
What if there are genuine health benefits that come along
for the ride? Might it be true that by focusing our efforts on
creating change, we also improve the states of our minds
and bodies? Could activism actually make us stronger?

This suggestion will likely come as a surprise to many.
After all, health practices and political activism usually
inhabit two completely different pigeonholes. Medicine is
all about disease, infection, antibiotics, physical exams, di-
agnosis, and treatment. Activism is all about politics, leg-
islation, organizing, fundraising, money, messaging, and
civil disobedience. They look like two completely different
challenges, with miles of empty space between them. But
what if we're wrong about all of this? What if activism isn't
just distantly related to medicine, but is actually integral to

health itself?

On the face of it, it might well seem that political activism doesn't have offer any of the familiar challenges we've come to associate with promoting good health. Holding up a sign on a street corner doesn't burn many calories; filing a petition or writing a letter doesn't build muscle. Go to a conference, testify in front of a committee, get arrested— these things sound stressful and maybe even health-negative. Who ever heard of someone going into activism specifically as a health practice?

But the value of activism lies in its integrating effect on the human organism. In this respect, the practice is very much akin to vigorous physical movement, otherwise known as exercise. When we act intentionally, particularly in the face of ambiguity and uncertainty, we call on the body-mind-spirit to gather its resources into a single, cohesive effort. This integrating effect can be powerfully health-positive, especially when we operate in the sweet spot of stress.

Poet and civil rights activist Audre Lorde recognized this clearly: "When I dare to be powerful, to use my strength in the service of my vision, then it becomes less and less important whether I am afraid."

THE SCIENCE

In fact, a growing body of evidence confirms the power of purpose and meaning in human health. In 2017, *New Scientist* magazine summarized the findings this way:

> People with a greater sense of purpose live longer,
> sleep better and have better sex. Purpose cuts the
> risk of stroke and depression. It helps people recover
> from addiction or manage their glucose levels if they

are diabetic. If a pharmaceutical company could bottle such a treatment, it would make billions.

And, coming at it from the opposite direction, we can say with confidence that *inactivism* is likely to be bad for our spirits and, in turn, our health. Across history and across the spectrum, writers and activists have described the perils of apathy and nonparticipation. As Martin Luther King, Jr., put it, "The way of acquiescence leads to moral and spiritual suicide." Likewise, Eleanor Roosevelt: "When you cease to make a contribution, you begin to die." And of course, conservationist Edward Abbey: "Sentiment without action is the ruin of the soul."

These elders are absolutely right: the failure to engage and participate is bad for our lives, and since everything in our lives and bodies is radically connected, it makes sense to suppose that inactivism will would have negative downstream consequences for the state of our bodies and our health.

A WHY TO LIVE

Naturally, this reminds us of Viktor Frankl and his legendary book *Man's Search for Meaning*. Incarcerated in a prisoner of war camp in World War II, Frankl saw suffering everywhere. Men were starving and freezing, and some literally worked to death; there was pain and misery in every moment. Some of the men buckled under the strain and perished early, but others managed to live and even to find fleeting moments of satisfaction in companionship. Frankl wondered, "Why do some survive while others weaken and die?"

His conclusion was that the survivors possessed a certain

sense of meaning and purpose that animated their lives and helped them transcend their suffering. He was fond of quoting the German philosopher Friedrich Nietzsche: "He who has a why to live can transcend almost any how." Or, we might say today, "He who has a why to live can tolerate almost any stressor."

This insight has a powerful appeal to those of us living in a hyperstressed environment, and it even suggests that having a "why" might well be the single most important factor in our well-being and our ability to manage the complexity of the modern world. Suddenly, all our obsessive focus on diet, exercise, and the other details of health begins to seem rather trivial and maybe even irrelevant. After all, none of the prisoners in Nazi concentration camps had anything resembling an optimal diet or exercise program. And yet, some of them managed to live and later thrive. Frankl himself lived to the age of ninety-two, animated, we can be sure, by his own powerful sense of why.

THE EUDAEMONIC WAY

Science confirms Frankl's experience. Steven Cole, a researcher at the University of California, Los Angeles, has spent years studying how negative experiences such as loneliness and stress can increase the expression of genes promoting inflammation and, in turn, disease. In his research, he compared two types of well-being: *hedonic*, that which comes from the pursuit of pleasure and rewards, and *eudaemonic*, that which comes from having a purpose beyond self-gratification.

The results were surprising: People with higher measures of hedonic well-being had higher expression of inflammatory genes and lower expression of genes for disease-fighting antibodies, a pattern also seen in loneliness and stress. For people scoring highest on eudaemonia, it was the opposite. Cole suspects that a focus on purpose decreases the nervous system's reaction to danger. Similar studies indicate that people with higher eudaemonic well-being have lower levels of the stress hormone cortisol. "Things that you value can override things that you fear," said Cole.

In other words, it's beginning to look like maximizing personal pleasure might not be the true path to health, stress-resistance, and sustainability. What we really need is a powerful purpose: a big why. The good news is that we already know how to do this. It's a human universal to be moved by the big whys of family, community, country, justice, and the quest for a better future. Intuitively, we seem to understand that life just works better when we focus on something bigger than ourselves.

Likewise, we begin to see that the self-focused why of modern culture is abnormal and historically deviant. A narcissistic sense of purpose can drive us for a time, but it ultimately turns ugly, dysfunctional, and irrelevant. Frankl would surely recognize the poverty of this kind of thinking and would have predicted the demise of any self-focused prisoners in his camp.

Instead, we need to keep our attention extended to the bigger circles of life. In particular, we need to connect our sense of meaning to our life-supporting systems, the biosphere, and the seventh generation, the legendary focal point for action in native cultures. These whys are important, not just for the benefits they bring to the systems and people in question, but because of the way they help us prevail in the face of chronic stress and uncertainty.

FINDING YOUR MEANING

For some of us, a sense of meaning and purpose comes easily. We come across it in our youth, or perhaps we're surrounded by people who are themselves acting on their own expansive sense of meaning. Maybe we're lucky enough to live in a community that's animated by an explicit sense of purpose. If so, you're ready to go forth.

But for others, a search may be required, and this will be a time for inquiry and introspection. Ask yourself:

What's the most important, meaningful, and relevant thing that I can do with my time on earth?

What will keep me moving forward when my life goes sideways?

What idea will sustain me when my activism runs into inevitable resistance, complexity, and setbacks?

What sense of purpose will pull me out of the quagmire of despair, depression, and resignation?

Or, to come at it from another direction: What kind of meaning and purpose would sustain me if I hit a financial jackpot and no longer had to worry about the practical necessities of life? Free and unburdened from rent, bills, and all the rest, what kinds of projects and missions would you take on? You could retire to a life of pleasure, but you can't imagine it because you've got more important things to do. Be audacious; choose something powerful, something that extends beyond the petty frictions and personal pleasures of routine human life. When it comes to a sense of meaning and purpose, bigger is always better.

FORGE THE BOND

Recognizing your meaning and purpose is a good first step, but this is not a passive, onetime exercise. It's not enough to simply point to a particular purpose and then carry on with your familiar daily life. Instead, you must strengthen the bond with repeated actions and inquiry. Take your activism out into the world and compare it with your sense of meaning. Are they congruent? Does one feed and reinforce the other? Keep asking and comparing. This will have a powerful, salutary effect on your entire mind-body-spirit. The closer you can get to living your meaning and purpose, the more powerful you'll become.

Above all, choose the biggest, most meaningful, most monumental struggles you can find. To be sure, this sounds crazy, and we might even say that only a fool would go out looking for an epic battle. Nevertheless, the prescription is sound. The classic struggles for justice, equality, peace, and a healthy human-habitat relationship are continuously challenging, and that's precisely the point. Epic battles offer the greatest benefit in meaning and purpose. They feed us with energy, and they help us integrate our powers. Don't waste your effort with trivial battles that sap your vitality. Instead, take on the biggest issues you can find. Your body and your spirit will thank you.

BEWARE THE DRAMA TRIANGLE

This is precisely the time when artists go to work. There is no time for despair, no place for self-pity, no need for silence, no room for fear...Like failure, chaos contains information that can lead to knowledge—even wisdom.

Toni Morrison

When all is well in our lives, it's easy to be patient and fair to the people around us. We're confident about who we are and where we stand. We take our time, exercise good judgment, and are tolerant of others. We're in control of our circumstances, and we might even feel creative and inspired.

But when we're under stress, all that goes out the window. Gradually or suddenly, our judgment becomes distorted. Emotions running high, we resort to blaming, complaining, faultfinding, evasions of responsibility, and desperate bids for rescue. *It's all his fault! They're the evildoers! I'm not to blame! Please come and fix me! Make my life work again!* These refrains have become so common in today's world that young people might suppose that they're normal human expressions; this is just how people talk.

But in fact, this is *not* how healthy people talk. These sentiments are symptoms of a dysfunctional attitude and relational pathology, first described by psychologist Stephen Karpman, in 1968. Often used as a tool in counseling and psychotherapy, Karpman's model has powerful applications across the entire range of human experience, including activism and martial artistry. It's called the *drama triangle.*

relational pathology, first described by psychologist Ste-

The trouble begins when a person identifies him or herself as a powerless *victim* in the face of circumstances. According to these self-declared victims, the source of their unhappiness lies outside themselves, with other people, agents, forces, and events. They pin the blame for their predicament on *persecutors,* or if that doesn't work, they go in search of *rescuers,* someone or some thing that will extract them from their trouble and save the day.

Of course, it's essential to remember there *are* genuine victims in this world and, just as obviously, authentic perpetrators who deserve justice. Likewise, there *are* times when we can and should reach out to others for support. But the drama triangle is about attitude, identity, and orientation. What role are we claiming in the world? Who is creating our lives? These are questions of agency and responsibility.

The drama begins when we're stressed, when we stumble, get hurt, or fail to get what we desire. Looking for a way out of our unhappiness, we identify ourselves as a powerless, innocent victim of circumstance. The source of suffering lies outside ourselves, with other people, agents, forces, and events. *It's someone else's fault that I'm suffering, not mine.* Instead of taking responsibility, we blame our parents, our genes, our childhood, our jobs, our bosses, and our partners. We blame humanity, society, government policy, the opposition party, stress, and, of course, the modern world itself.

These accusations may well contain elements of truth, but this is beside the point. The real issue is our orientation. By claiming the role of victim, we give away our power. No longer are we acting in the world—the world is acting on us. Suddenly, our identity is compromised, and we're hamstrung by our beliefs. This makes our activism and our martial artistry far more difficult, and maybe even impossible. Once we define ourselves as victims, it's hard to find a way forward.

Going to the other point of the triangle—toward rescue—is not much better. In our unhappiness, we look for people, substances, ideas, habits, or organizations to bail us out of our predicament. But once again, we give away our power. Rescuers can sometimes comfort us, agree with us, and maybe even go to battle and solve some problems for us, but none of this really helps. In the long run, we discover that our predicament still exists, and nothing has really changed. We haven't discovered a sense of agency, and if anything, we're more dependent and weaker than before.

A HUMAN UNIVERSAL?

Many of us have heard this story before, and it's easy to assume that the victim orientation is something reserved for the dark underbelly of society—hardened alcoholics, drug addicts, and criminals come to mind. But victimhood is alive and well at every level, and no one is immune. In fact, drama might well be a human universal, a common reaction of all people who are under stress.

That's because drama is an easy, seductive trap. There's always plenty of blame to go around; perpetrators are everywhere, and excuses are always handy. The economy is in recession, our parents were flawed, our neighborhood was in turmoil, and on it goes. Immigrants took our jobs, bullies abused us, schools failed us, and the system didn't provide the kinds of opportunities we deserved.

In the process, complaining has now become a national sport, with entire media empires dedicated to round-the-clock finger-pointing, otherwise known as "blamestorming." When things aren't going well, there's always a perpetrator we can blame, right across the aisle, across the border, or down the street.

It gets worse. When we're highly stressed, it becomes easier and more tempting to cast blame on others. In the process, we become increasingly susceptible to any handy narrative, no matter how preposterous, as long as it suits our purposes. No conspiracy theory is too outlandish, no leap of faith too extreme. If it helps us build a case against our chosen perpetrator, we're all in. And before long, we stop cross-checking, stop seeking truth, and stop asking deeper questions about evidence, sources, facts, and history.

It takes a good deal of cognitive labor and strength of character to examine propositions in detail, to dig for scientific truth, and to revise our understandings. But when we're overwhelmed and exhausted, we have no energy for such projects: it's easier to simply blame whomever or whatever's handy.

Worse yet, the drama is highly contagious. When we see people around us blaming perpetrators and running for rescue, the behavior becomes normalized and familiar, even expected. We come to believe that's just how it's done in human society and, before long, millions of people are working the drama triangle full-time. In theory, we could find our way out of this mess by accepting responsibility and actively creating our lives, but this requires character and resolve, qualities that are in increasingly short supply in our stressed-out world.

ESCAPE THE DRAMA TRIANGLE

In theory at least, avoiding the chaos and disempowerment of the drama triangle is simple. As thousands of therapists, coaches, and other smart people have advised, the way out is by accepting responsibility and getting back to work on your chosen project or path. In other words, *create your way out*. Start by focusing on what you're trying to build, and keep your attention trained on your objectives. Ignore the perpetrators and forget about rescue. When you've got your sights set on a worthy goal, you simply won't have time for blaming, complaining, or whining; you've got important work to do.

For the activist, this reframe is powerful. Suddenly you'll realize that the so-called perpetrators in your life are no longer such potent adversaries. In fact, they might even be irrelevant. This frees up immense amounts of psycho-spiritual energy that can be used to create the kind of life you're after and to fight the essential battles that need to be fought.

The same goes for rescue. When you're immersed in a creative endeavor, you no longer feel the need to be propped up or saved from suffering. Genuine support will always be welcome, but rescue is a distraction. Your work keeps you engaged, focused, and integrated.

REMEMBER...

Going forward, remember to stay alert to your orientation, your attitude, and your identity. It's easy to get sucked back into the drama triangle, and you'll probably revert back to old habits on occasion, but don't take the bait. Embrace responsibility and stay focused on your creative work. Next time you hear yourself blaming, complaining, or wishing for someone to save you, wake up and listen to your language. There's a creative project out there with your name on it. Get to work.

TREAT PEOPLE LIKE ANIMALS

We must, however, acknowledge, as it seems to me, that man with all his noble qualities…still bears in his bodily frame the indelible stamp of his lowly origin.

Charles Darwin

As an activist and martial artist, you're going to find yourself immersed in some tricky and ambiguous situations. Conditions will often be demanding, and you'll be risking your time, your attention, your career, maybe even your life on an uncertain process and outcome. The experience may well ask more from you than you thought possible.

In other words, you're going to be under stress. Not only will you yourself be feeling the heat, you'll also be working with people and organizations that are themselves stretched to the limit. Stress is now an ever-present feature of the modern world, and the human animal is scrambling to adapt. We see the evidence everywhere: rudeness and uncivil behavior, air rage, road rage, school board confrontations, decreasing social trust, and increasing polarization, all of it coupled with high levels of suspicion and anxiety. People are on edge.

In one sense, the lives of our hunting and gathering ancestors were easy. To be sure, there were lethal dangers on the grassland, but these dangers were immediate, and even somewhat predictable. A person could understand the threats posed by carnivores and other large animals, fire, cliffs, swift water, snakes, and occasional attacks by neighboring tribes. In turn, these understandings could be embedded in an oral tradition and passed from generation to generation.

But, today, the advance of civilization has multiplied perceived dangers a thousandfold, and now we're faced with myriad threats, not all of them visible, predictable, or even understandable: computer viruses, real viruses, collapsing supply chains, and constantly shifting economic conditions keep us stuck on high alert. In short, modern humans are suffering under a stress burden that's unprecedented in our history. And even worse, the challenge is chronic—precisely the formula for lifestyle disease, compromised performance, and bad behavior.

THINK OF YOUR ADVERSARY

The standard wellness narrative tells us that stress is bad for our health, and if we want to live a long life, we need to keep it in check with familiar stress-management techniques. Coaches, trainers, and therapists point to a standard suite of remedies that include exercise, meditation, good sleep, and social support. All have been proven beneficial, and all can play an important role in promoting the quality of our lives.

But for the activist, our modern understanding also has a great deal to say about how we interact with those around us, particularly our adversaries. Specifically, it suggests that we craft our messages and actions with an eye for how stressed our "target audience" might happen to be.

In turn, this brings us to an essential reframe. Most of us are accustomed to thinking of our adversaries as people, but knowing what we now know about biology, it might be better to step back and think about them as animals. After all, our adversaries are products of evolution, and they've got an immense amount in common with every other primate that's ever lived. They may well be misguided, confused, power-mad, or corrupt, but they're still animals.

This gives the activist a powerful perspective and a new way to look at his or her actions, presentations, and pitches. Specifically, the challenge is to look at our adversaries and think about what's going on in their bodies, especially their autonomic nervous systems. Will my action trigger a fight-flight response and a hostile counter-reaction? Or will it move them into a more receptive rest-and-digest way of being? Will my actions engage them in the sweet spot of stress—that productive domain of experience where humans tend to perform at their best? Or will it push them past the tipping point into the red zone of hyperstress and militant opposition?

In all likelihood, you've never thought of activism in these terms. You just want to win. You want to advance your agenda, present your demands, make your case, and defeat your enemy. You might even be thinking, *Who cares what's going on in my adversary's body? If he's overstressed, that's his problem.* But the time has come for more sophistication and attention. Knowing the state of your animal adversary will go a long way towards determining your success or failure as an activist and a human being.

CHALLENGE, ASK, OR THREAT?

Just imagine that there's something you want, from some-one who's resistant to giving it to you. How do you pitch it? What kind of messaging makes the most biological sense? Are you making a request? A threat? An ask? Or a demand?

This might seem to be a matter of mere semantics, but from the animal's point of view, the form of your pitch makes a big difference. If your presentation comes across as too soft, there won't be a stress response in your adver-sary at all, but if it's too threatening, the fight-flight re-sponse kicks in, and your adversary will either shut down or retaliate.

In fact, research shows that the human body reacts in very different ways, depending on whether the stressor is experienced as a challenge or a threat. Work by June Gruber at Yale University shows that when conditions are perceived as challenging, a host of beneficial physiological consequences follow: increased cardiac output, increased diameter of circulatory vessels, increased blood flow to the brain, and, most notably, increased cognitive and phys-ical performance. But when conditions are perceived as threatening, it all goes the other way: physiology and per-formance both enter a state of contraction, which, in turn, makes people resistant to change.

All of which suggests that we should craft our actions and pitches with the animal in mind. For example, it's often said that "power yields nothing without a demand," but it's also true that hardball ultimatums are inherently stress-provok-ing and might well be counterproductive. Just imagine how *you* feel when someone comes to you with a demand for action. Are you going to be receptive, or are you going to

close the gates and lock the doors? Your adversary probably feels exactly the same way.

Of course, there's plenty of variation and dynamism here,
and success will always depends on the state of the animal
in question. Naturally, homework and attention are crucial.
Study your adversary and take note of their stress history.
Are they in a state of power and privilege? Or are they up
against a wall? Are they up to their eyeballs in cognitive
overload, competing demands, and time pressures? If so,
you might have better luck by offering up a relaxed and
casual approach; if you can find a way to ease your adversary's stress load, he might even be excited to talk. In any
case, inquiry is key. Whatever the stress conditions of your
adversary, try to move them into the sweet spot—the place
where progress is possible.

POWER AND MORAL STRESS

On the flip side, what if your adversary is already in a relaxed state of mind and body? For example, people of power and privilege are largely insulated against stress of all
kinds. They've built protective structures around their lives
and have the luxury of doing more or less as they please. If
things get too stressful, they can buy their way out of trouble or tap into networks of other powerful people. In other
words, they've got a greater sense of control and, in turn, a
more relaxed state of being.

This calls for a different kind of inquiry and strategy. Specifically, *How do I amplify the stress on someone who's already protected, insulated, and heavily resourced?* Conventional appeals to financial or political consequences might
not get you anywhere at all. Unless you represent a large

number of voters or can wield vast sums of money, your appeals might well fall on deaf ears.

But perhaps you can bring some moral or ethical stress to bear. Even the most hardened politicians and corporate leaders have a lingering sense of decency and might even think of themselves as benevolent actors. Can you appeal to their humanity? Can you show them the human consequences of their current behavior?

Tell them about the suffering that will come to their children and grandchildren in coming years. Tell them what their position on habitat, forests, and oceans means for real people. Turn up the heat, and appeal to conscience. You may not get the ultimate solution you desire, but you might find some common ground and a chance for further engagement.

KEEP YOUR EYE ON THE ANIMAL

In any case, keep your attention trained on the human body, and be alert for signs of contentment, ease, distress, or incipient panic. Study human postures, facial expressions, tones of voice, cadences of speech, and any other qualities that might offer clues that might to the state of a person's autonomic nervous system. You won't always understand the complete picture, but any insight at all will give you a substantial advantage. When it comes to working with primates under pressure, knowledge of the autonomic system is power.

TELL A BETTER STORY

We can complain because rose bushes have thorns,
or rejoice because thorns have roses.

Alphonse Karr
A Tour Round My Garden

The future is made of choices. Hundreds of times each day, we choose one thing over another, making small and large decisions as we go, creating our lives and the lives of others in the process. Across humanity, people make uncountable billions of decisions every hour, every day, year after year. If we could shift the tide of these decisions even slightly, the end result would be a significant, even massive shift in the trajectory of our world.

But the decisions we make do not come out of thin air. We choose one thing over another because of our values, but those values are driven by culture, which, in turn, is driven by story. If you really want to change the future, a good place to begin is with the stories we tell ourselves and each other about the world and how it works.

Storytelling is familiar to all of us, but because it's so familiar, we tend to forget how powerful it really is. As with so many other elements of human life, we develop a kind of amnesia about things that we grow up with—and in the process, go blind to some of the most important forces in our lives.

In fact, story is one of the most potent forces on the

planet. Story holds the master ideas of a culture. It gives us power or takes it away. It gives us a sense of priority and helps us navigate the tough judgment calls that we face each day. In essence, our lives are made of story.

The beauty of story is that it's easy to understand and connects directly with the human experience. It bypasses rational, cognitive labor and appeals directly to the imagination. When story works, it gives us a sense of clarity about our lives and can even connect us to the extraordinary forces that animate our bodies and our spirits.

THE STATE OF STORY

Sadly, the state of story in the modern world is chaos. Formerly a powerful force for cultural focus and meaning, story has devolved into a means of passive entertainment and, of course, profit. Over the last several decades, we've grown accustomed to the notion that the primary purpose of story is to keep us amused. A story is considered "good" if it keeps our attention for the duration of the telling—and if it "captures eyeballs," as the marketers put it, so much the better.

All of which is historically unprecedented. In the Paleolithic world of hunting and gathering, story was absolutely critical to survival and tribal function. People coalesced around a small number of narratives, repeated often. People told stories of animals, people, hunting, and the cosmos at large, but these stories were far more than entertainment. They explained the world and held people together. Everyone in your tribe would have known the master narratives of your culture; you heard the stories almost every night, and you slept well, secure in the knowledge that life made some kind of sense.

But today we're suffering from an avalanche of fragmented narratives—a million swirling and overlapping stories, each describing some narrow facet of reality or the human experience, all of them competing with one another for the last remaining fragments of human attention. Today we have an astronomical glut of stories, but they come and go with the wind, and rarely do they hang around long enough to bring us together.

Even worse, our modern storytelling landscape is populated by a glut of plastic narratives—inauthentic, artificial nuggets of guidance about how to live, brought to us by corporate marketing departments. These "life lessons" are massively premeditated, focus-group tested, and produced. They tell us how to look, train, work, love, value, and experience life. Like fast food, these highly polished narratives are easy to consume, but tragically, they displace the authentic human stories that we so desperately need.

Modern storytelling also fails to address the most urgent problems of our age. Aside from apocalyptic disaster films and books, modern narratives rarely have anything useful to say about the destruction of the biosphere or the dysfunctional state of human-nature relations. In other words, we're living in the midst of a "myth gap," a profound and disturbing disconnect between our predicament and the stories that we tell one another.

The problem with the myth gap is not just its failure to guide us, but also that it leaves us exposed to distraction and toxic, corrosive myths that erode our health, our lives, and our future. Without a guiding narrative, we become vulnerable to whatever story happens to be making the rounds, putting us at the mercy of whoever's got the biggest megaphone. Our attention and identities are captured by plastic narratives that mainly serve the teller, rarely if ever the listener.

THE PRACTICE OF NARRATIVE ACTIVISM

Conditioned by conventional culture, many activists are quick to assume that the only way to make a difference is through the use of conventional power and social force. Get the right academic degree, go to law school, ascend to the right government or corporate position, and start wielding power. But no matter your rank in a hierarchy, story remains an essential element in the process. Crafting and sharing the right narrative at the right time can make the difference between failure and success. As activists, story is implicit in everything we do. No matter the details of our protests, blockades, or civil disobedience, there's always a set of assumptions and expectations that's wrapped up in the doing. In this sense, *all* activism is narrative in nature.

So how do we wield our narrative powers? How do we talk to the media, to our audiences, and to people who might have some leverage? How should we talk to our allies and our adversaries? Obviously, you'd like your listeners to hear your story and maybe even adopt your perspective on the issue in question. But before you put your fingers to the keyboard or sit yourself down in front of a webcam, it's essential to circle back and review your methods and objectives.

TAKE CONTROL OF THE NARRATIVE

The first step is to take control of the narrative. Obviously, this is no easy task, especially when your opponent has a larger megaphone. But opportunities will arise, so be prepared with a simple, coherent presentation. Refine your narrative in advance, be clear and persistent, and, whatever you do, stay on message. When your adversary attempts to steer the conversation in another direction, don't be intimidated into accepting his assumptions and framing. Stay calm and on point. Turn the conversation back to your objective, over and over again as necessary. Obviously, this will require some persistence and fortitude, but stick with it. Your perspective matters, and your voice deserves to be heard.

STRETCH THE OVERTON WINDOW

On the face of it, narrative activism means making a case for the kind of change you'd like to see in the world, but to put it another way, what you're really trying to do is expand the scope of conversation around the issue in question. Specifically, you'd like your audience to stretch their conversation to include your perspective. In other words, you're trying to open up the "Overton window" of discourse.

This idea refers to the range of policies that are politically acceptable to mainstream culture at a given time. According to the theory, there are six degrees of acceptance for ideas that lie outside the conventional realm of discourse: In the beginning, an idea is considered unthinkable, then radical, then acceptable, then sensible, then popular, then, finally, established policy.

There's a good lesson here. That is, you're not just working your issue, you're also working with popular imagination and culture at large. Pushing a so-called radical idea might seem to go nowhere, but it might well expand the dialogue. You might not succeed in the details, but if you're persistent, you might open up the conversation for future proposals.

For example, you might well believe that nonhuman animals and habitat are entitled to certain rights, and you support the modern rights of nature movement. So far, so good, but most conventionalists find the idea to be either unthinkable or extreme. You can't change their minds in an instant, so persistence is vital. The very fact that you've got people talking is a powerful first step. As more people join in the conversation, your ideas may come to be seen as more palatable, less radical, and maybe even sensible and popular. Don't give up.

BEWARE MILITANT LANGUAGE

As you craft your narratives, be particularly careful with militant language and military metaphors. In our passion for change, we're often inclined to see everything through the lenses of conflict, opposition, and extremes; a thing is either this way or that way, you're either with us or against us. Everyone is either an ally or an adversary, a force for good or a force for evil. There's no middle ground, no hybrids, and no complementary relationships.

To be sure, militant language feels good and sometimes has its place, but it can also lead to premature polarization by forcing people into corners and pigeonholes. This inflames relationships that might well be on their way to resolution. Militant language over-simplifies complex realities and can even polarize things that may not really need to be polarized. When your language destroys the middle ground, it can be hard to go back.

Even worse, militant language is extremely contagious. Every time we hear polarizing statements, we're more likely to adopt similar black-and-white perspectives. And in short order, everyone is locked into either-or orientations, which only increases the adversarial energy in the system. Is this what you want? Do you really want to force a highly complex reality into a polarized, adversarial form? Maybe it's better to save the militant language as a last resort.

THE USE AND ABUSE OF CARTOONS

Stories move us, entertain us, tear us apart, and sometimes even heal us. But it would be a mistake to suppose that stories must take the form of sustained, in-depth narratives. Cartoons are stories too, and they can tell us a great deal about relationships, ideas, and dimensions of the human experience, sometimes in extremely powerful ways.

The beauty of a good cartoon is that it takes us straight to the emotion, the meaning, or the insight. It's a simplification that strips away complications and unnecessary detail. This allows the brain to go directly to the heart of the matter with minimal cognitive effort. Cartoons guide our attention and, in turn, our intelligence. In a sense, we see through our cartoons.

Simplicity gives cartoons their power and appeal, but it also makes them dangerous. If we get our cartoons right, we reveal profound truths to the world, but if we get them wrong, we wreak havoc and chaos. Cartoons become caricature, caricature becomes stereotype, stereotype becomes ideology, ideology becomes dogma. When we take this path, our cartoonish, hyper-simplified world views no longer reveal truth, but rather obscure it. By eliminating detail and nuance, they put us in danger for polarization, grid-lock, and stupidity.

So what's the art? How do we become more effective and sensible cartoonists? As usual, the practice begins with awareness. Our biggest problem is that we're careless. The simplicity of cartoons subverts our intelligence. In conversation, we toss off generalizations without thinking; we broad-brush people, events, and the world at large. We leave out mountains of nuance. Uncomfortable with the rich, squirming ambiguity of the world and its vast, almost unimaginable scope, we drive straight to what we think might be the point.

Likewise, be wary of statements built on simplistic causality—cartoons that suggest a single cause leading to a single effect. We hear these over-simplified explanations throughout popular culture: one gene causes one disease or personality trait, one dietary nutrient causes one physiological result, one brain region is responsible for one behavior, one political act has a particular social consequence. All these cartoons lead us astray and ultimately limit our understanding. Don't fall for them.

Above all, slow your stories down; it takes time to describe the myriad relationships that surround people, events, and ideas. Use cartoons to learn, grow, explore, entertain, and enlighten. Don't use them to coerce, obscure, tyrannize, or control. Be alert for those great linguistic simplifiers: *all, never, every, none, everyone, no one,* and especially *is* and *are.* When you hear or speak with these broad brushes, you might well be dealing with a cartoon. (As author Wendell Johnson jokingly put it, "Always and never are two words you should always remember never to use.")

NARRATIVE LEADERSHIP...

Ultimately, the cure for bad stories is better stories. For the narrative activist, this means exercising leadership in the midst of chaos and conflict. Cut through the clutter by pointing out dysfunctional stories and dangerous, outdated narratives. If necessary, interrupt the conversation and show a better way. In particular, share narratives of interdependence, humility, and intimacy with the natural world. If you want to move the world, move the narrative.

PUT YOUR BODY WHERE YOUR MOUTH IS

The world is changed by your example, not by your opinion.

Novelist Paulo Coelho

As we've seen, story is one of the most powerful tools in the activist's collection. Those who can speak and write most effectively are likely to succeed in creating social, ecological, and cultural change. But there's even more to the story, you might say, because language also has a powerful impact, not just on our ability to communicate with one another, but also on the ways we define and experience our personal lives.

On the face of it, it might well seem that words and actions belong to two distinctly different domains: language is one thing, action another. Words are just sounds in the air, marks on the page, or lights on the screen. Sometimes they're entertaining, sometimes enlightening, or sometimes just noisy. And on some days, it might even seem that we can ignore them altogether.

But the words we speak reveal important facts about our character, especially when coupled with action. To put it another way, the story-behavior connection is vital to who we are and what we might become. As the fourteenth-century Persian poet Hafiz put it, "The words you speak become the house you live in."

If you're like most people, you want others to listen to you, to care about what you say, and maybe even respect your ideas. In short, you want to be taken seriously. But when we fail to walk our talk—when we say one thing and do another—the consequences can be severe and wide ranging. To our listeners, we come across as insincere blowhards and bloviators. Our words don't ring true, and people will quickly dismiss us and everyone who looks like us. In other words, it doesn't matter how fluent you are; *the real persuasion lies in the congruence between words and deeds.*

This is particularly true in the world of leadership, where it's just not enough to simply "talk the talk." Followers pay close attention, not just to the language of their leaders, but to the totality of their lives. Listeners are alert to empty words and are quick to judge any disconnects. When leaders display high congruence between their walk and their talk, people are likely to accept the message and follow along. *If he can do it, so can I.*

THE POWER OF CONGRUENCE

When we're infants, we babble. Words are cheap, easy, and rarely consequential. They're just noises that sometimes have meaning attached, but we really don't pay much attention to how they match up with the rest of our lives. We express ourselves on impulse, while our ancient animal bodies make their own decisions and generate their own behaviors.

At this point in life, nobody cares much about your walk-talk ratio; no one really expects children to be true to their words. But little by little, our disconnects start to get us into trouble, sometimes big trouble. By the time we enter the adult world, the people around us expect consistency in our words and action, and get angry when we fail to live up to our language. This realization marks—or should mark—our transition into adulthood. It moves us towards integrity, but at the same time, it also moves us towards personal power and agency. In essence, walk-talk integration is the very foundation of character.

This is precisely the point made by Don Miguel Ruiz in his book *The Four Agreements*. The first agreement is simple: "Be impeccable with your word." Monitor your talk and compare it with your walk. Are there disconnects? Can you move them closer together? By closing the gap between walk and talk, we move closer to maturity, integration, and, in turn, effectiveness. Before long, people will start listening to what you say.

For the activist, there's a discipline here, driven by a simple resolution: *"I'm not going to advocate for something I'm not willing to do."* In other words, if you're not willing to walk it, don't talk it. If you're advocating for reduced consumption of fossil fuels and cutting back on flying, you'd better be cutting back on flying. If you're advocating for a vegan diet, you'd better not be eating meat. If you're advocating for "radical action" and "aggressive civil disobedience," to bring down the system, you'd better be willing to get arrested.

CHANGE THE TALK, CHANGE THE WALK

Listen to your words. Can you live up to your language? If not, change your walk or change your talk. Not just every now and then, but every day. *"How is my behavior holding up next to my language?"* By asking this question, we move closer and closer to integration and, in the process, the thing we recognize as character. In turn, our activism and our personal lives become increasingly meaningful and powerful.

THE ART IS LONG

The eyes of the future are looking back at us and
they are praying for us to see beyond our own time.

Terry Tempest Williams

The years go by, and we fight, over and over, for what we
believe and what we love. We fight for our life-supporting systems, our planet, one another, and for some kind
of a functional future. Sometimes we win small victories,
but the odds are long and defeat is common. We strive and
suffer, throwing all our effort into battle, but little seems
to change. Looking at the brutal evidence of climate chaos
and extinction, it's easy to fall back into the quagmire of depression, nihilism, and misanthropy. Therapists tell us that
the antidote to despair is action, but even the most concentrated efforts often fall short, and we find ourselves back at
square one, worrying about the misery that's to come.

But it's essential to remember that much of our suffering
is based on the fact that we're measuring our effectiveness
against the spans of our short, individual lives. We work
on an issue for months or years, and at the end, the world
doesn't look much different than it did before, and maybe
even worse. Our efforts haven't moved the needle on the
world, so what's the point? But perhaps our thinking is too
short, our timelines too limited, our attention too myopic.
Instead of thinking in terms of months and years, maybe
we can find some perspective and equanimity by stretching

our time horizon deeper into the future. Maybe a longer view will yield something a little more meaningful, tolerable, and functional.

PLAY A LONGER GAME

Try extending your thinking beyond the span of your individual life, all the way out to the seventh generation. Can you see yourself planting seeds that will sprout a hundred or even a thousand years from now? What if you're working for people, plants, and animals that are yet to be? What if your job description stretches well beyond the reach of a conventional career?

Suddenly, certain adversities become easier to bear. A short-term defeat is simply that—a small setback in a much larger game. When you're working for the future, bad days are to be expected, so there's less cause for concern. This long view can be a powerful tonic for the stressed-out activist. You're less likely to get stuck in the struggles of the day, and you're more likely to act with a greater sense of meaning and purpose. And, paradoxically, you're likely to be more effective.

When playing a long game, we spend less time thinking about defense and the outrageous behavior of our adversaries and more time thinking about what our descendants might actually need. Yes, of course, some of our opponents are true criminal actors who are destroying our planet and our future. Yes, their behavior should be contained and punished. But, in the long game, we spend more of our time focusing on creation. You've got a goal, an objective, and a target, and even if that target lies beyond the life of your individual body, it's still worth focusing on and fighting for.

This is intergenerational activism.

Of course, to make this perspective work, you've got to get out of your narrow self-interest and stop thinking about personal rewards that might come to you because of your work. Ultimately, this isn't about you; it's about your descendants. The future people who will benefit from your efforts won't be able to reward you, and you'll be lucky if they even remember you at all. They might honor their ancestors in some way, but you'll be long gone. That's just the nature of this work.

This perspective suggests that we focus less on the success or failure of today's battle and instead start asking ourselves, *"What will the seventh generation need to survive and thrive?"* Suddenly, things become clear, and some of our stress starts to fade away. We see that the seventh generation needs healthy habitat, fresh water, a functional atmosphere, biodiversity, a functional culture, and a unifying narrative. And that's a good start. If you fight for these things—even in some small measure—you're doing good work.

FOCUS ON THE JOURNEY

This long view shifts our focus away from the destination and back onto the quality of our journey. In a butterfly world, we can't really control results, but we can control the way we show up. We can't control what effects our work will have on future generations, but we can control our stance, our pace, our resolve, and our focus.

The trick, as always, is to get your spirit right. Fight the battles that need to be fought, but disconnect your happiness from short-term outcomes. Above all, don't limit your participation to battles that promise a perfect end result. Instead, engage on principle and act on purpose. As the writer Chris Hedges put it, "I don't fight because I think I'm going to win. I fight because it's the right thing to do."

Likewise, Native American activist Russell Means, speaking when heavily outnumbered by federal agents at Wounded Knee in 1972, said: "We are not concerned with winning or losing, nor are we concerned about the odds against us. We're here because it's the right thing to do and the right place to be."

To be sure, destinations and objectives matter, but some things are worth doing for their own sake. As the Czech dissident and statesman Václav Havel put it, "Hope is not the conviction that something will turn out well, but the certainty that something is worth doing no matter how it turns out."

REMEMBER THIS...

Ultimately, it's our fortitude that will carry us forward into the future. This spirit is the defining quality of the activist and the legacy that he or she leaves to the world. As the eco-anarchist Edward Abbey put it, "Without courage, all other virtues are useless." Yes, hard days are to come, but keep your eyes focused on the quality and integrity of the journey.

WE ARE SO FOCUSED

The sacred function of leaders is to remain awake.

Roger Hallam

Welsh environmental activist

Co-founder of Extinction Rebellion

So concludes our journey out of the quagmire, from *We Are So Fucked* to *We Are So Focused*. Conditions are still as challenging as ever, and new threats lie just over the horizon, but now you've got some perspective and ideas for moving forward. The biosphere is still in grave danger, and the prognosis remains challenging, but now you've got a path, a sense of direction and agency. You're becoming an activist and a martial artist.

TURN IT AROUND

No matter your skill and judgment, the path ahead will be arduous. You're going to suffer defeats, and you'll have to endure the sufferings of friends, allies, and the plants, animals, and habitat of the natural world. Along the way, you might well get sucked back into the abyss of hopelessness, despair, and depression. You're going to have bad days, bad months, even bad years.

But there are ways to maintain your resolve and keep yourself in the game. Remind yourself that you're doing good work. You're a creative person fighting uphill against entrenched cultural forces and long-standing inertia. In this effort, resistance is inevitable. In fact, the stress and exhaustion that you're experiencing is a sign that you're doing something right.

Defeats are hard to suffer, but they can also inspire. The predicament, onerous as it is, can be a paradoxical fuel for your efforts. The trick is to turn your mind around and transform your adversity into a source of power. Rewire your reactions and your spirit; reverse the polarity of your hardships. Turn energy sucks into energy sources, distraction into concentration. Turn trauma, pain, and frustration into resolve. Turn your anger into targeted, intentional actions.

Obviously, you can only go so far with this kind of reframing. After all, the animal body is ultimately in charge, and negative experiences will have their say. But there is room to maneuver, and experience can often be reinterpreted. Successful people do this all the time.

We've all heard the adage that "Whatever doesn't kill me makes me stronger." It's a powerful idea, but even better is "Whatever doesn't kill me gives me focus." Or, better yet, from the 2020 hit song "Counting Stars" by OneRepublic, "Everything that kills me makes me feel alive." Your adversity, pain, and suffering can actually inspire you to redouble your efforts. In this way, dark experience can actually motivate. This psycho-spiritual judo is not just a clever mind trick, it's a genuinely creative act and is vitally important work for every activist. Going forward, this is the work of our day and our age.

Of course, you're going to screw up along the way and you're going to make some wicked mistakes. You'll exercise poor judgment, misread conditions, and go down the wrong paths. You'll make sincere efforts, over and over, and you'll still find ways to get it wrong. All of which hurts like hell, but it's to be expected. You're just one primate trying to get a grasp on an immensely complex butterfly world. Just when you think you've got a solid understanding, that's when the surprises will come to visit.

So don't be dismayed. No one really knows how to "do activism." No one really knows how to transform a massively entrenched system in crisis. You're working in uncharted historical waters, and you can't be expected to get it all right. Don't let your mistakes and missteps pull you back into the quagmire. Error is not wrong. On the contrary, it's the path, the way. Error is your teacher, your coach, your counselor. As the French philosopher Albert Camus put it, "One recognizes one's course by discovering the paths that stray from it." There's nothing to be ashamed of here.

YOUR INVISIBLE ALLIES

There are going to be times when you'll feel alone, isolated, and exposed. You might even come to believe that you're an outlier in society and that you're surrounded by people who don't know about our predicament or don't care. On some days, the alienation is going to be brutal. You'll reach for connection and common ground, only to be met with a handful of platitudes, trivia, denial, and useless hope.

Do not lose heart and above all, don't stop caring. In a fundamental sense, you *are* different. The fact that you feel isolated is nothing to be ashamed of. Rather, it's evidence of your concern, your maturity, and your willingness to accept responsibility. Your path will not be easy, but remember this: you do have allies, scattered across the globe. At this very moment, millions of people are working for a functional future in whatever way they can. You may not see them or hear from them, but they exist and they're grappling with the same kinds of issues you are. These people know the state of the planet and are committed to action. Like you, they accept responsibility and are willing to stand up for the future. Don't forget this.

ONE MORE GRAIN

Perhaps a metaphor from the world of science history will help. Prior to the 1960s, most people thought of scientific progress as the simple accumulation of knowledge; new evidence builds on the established structure, brick by brick, fact by fact, one journal article stacked upon another. The process seemed pretty linear and maybe even boring, but in 1962, the philosopher Thomas Kuhn told us a different, highly disruptive story. In his classic work *The Structure of Scientific Revolutions*, he argued for a dynamic model in which periods of stasis are interrupted by episodes of revolutionary discovery and re-imagining.

The process begins with the appearance of minor, inconvenient anomalies that seem to contradict the dominant paradigm. At the outset, this countervailing evidence goes largely ignored and may even be ridiculed. No one pays much attention, but over time, the weight of evidence accumulates, leading to a sudden and dramatic shift in thinking and attention: the famous *paradigm shift*.

In essence, Kuhn argued that the process of scientific and cultural change operates like an enormous balance scale. The scientist or activist adds a contradictory idea to one side, but nothing seems to happen. The process continues for some time, and during this period, he or she may well conclude that his or her efforts are having no effect. Thus the despair.

But the grains of sand do add up, and shifts do come, sometimes in an instant. Long periods of apparent stasis can be interrupted by swift, even breathtaking transformations. In fact, this process is consistent with the findings of political scientist Erica Chenoweth and her "3.5% rule of social change." Working with researchers at the International Center on Nonviolent Conflict, Chenoweth performed an extensive review of civil resistance and social movements in the twentieth century and discovered that it only takes a small shift in people's attitudes to make a substantial difference. She also discovered that nonviolent campaigns are twice as likely to succeed as violent campaigns. These findings have been instrumental in inspiring the work of Extinction Rebellion, Scientist Rebellion, and other activist groups.

All of which encourages us to stay in the fight. The grain of sand you drop upon the scale may look and feel invisible, but it is not nothing. You may not see the effect, even in your lifetime, but the scales will move as people add their grains of effort and courage. Sooner or later, the paradigm will shift, and the shift may be bigger, faster, and more significant than we think.

In other words, small increments matter. Don't fall into the all-or-nothing trap, the black-and-white perspective that says, "It's either victory or defeat." *In a butterfly world, every effort matters.* Even in defeat, we may well be moving ideas and culture in ways that are invisible to us. Small victories, even microscopic victories, are something. Every acre of habitat saved matters. Every species, every animal, every plant, every life. As Greta Thunberg put it, "Every fraction of a degree matters." Save what you can, as much as you can, when you can. The tipping point may be closer than you think.

Your results might feel like nothing, but in the end, your effort is sacred.

GRATITUDE AND APPRECIATION

How many keystrokes and mouse clicks does it take to save the planet? I'm not sure I know the answer, but I think it must be a very large number, multiplied by even larger numbers. And so it's been for me on this project. Day after day, sweating under yet another brutal heat dome in the northwest of Turtle Island, I made a go of it. Write a page, then delete it in a spasm of confusion. Rearrange the outline, then panic with the realization that there are probably an infinite number of ways to say anything. Write more, edit more, give up hope, then try again.

On some days, it felt like every keystroke was a gesture of irrelevance, an awkward groping into the void. Would my words ever make it into print? Would anyone care if I said one thing rather than another? And if they did, would my language move their hearts, minds, and behavior? Would my readers actually go on to move the needle on the world? Was I being relevant or simply naive?

Doubt and confusion are never far away in the writer's life. On good days, the words flow freely, fluently, and coherently, but otherwise, it's a psycho-spiritual battle of wills. The adversary within can be relentless, diabolical, and unforgiving. No sentence, no phrase, no line of reasoning is ever good enough. Whatever it is, it could always be better.

The good news is that I've been supported by a powerful group of allies along the way. In particular, my immense gratitude goes to Derrick Jensen and Marisa Solis, my editorial wizard. Likewise, I've received vital inspirations and gestures of support from Susan Fahringer, Michael Dowd, Alessandro Pelizzon, Steve Laskevitch and Carla Fraga, Corey Jung, Sebastien Alary and Anne Smith, Paul Landon, Skye Nacel, Steve Myrland and Kellie Murphy, Dr. Rodney King, Will Heckman, Jonathan Logan, John Hagar, Barb Moro and Diedre Knowlton, Louie and Gerlinde Gelina, Pete Karabetis, Michael Campi, Max Wilbert, Lierre Kieth, Will Falk, and all my professors and martial art teachers. And most of all, the love of my life, Sue Schwantes.